IMAGES
of America

THE KENTUCKY
BOURBON TRAIL

MEN AND MASH TUBS. This photograph was taken at the Herbst Distillery in 1905. The distillery near Frankfort produced Old Judge Bourbon and Old Fitzgerald Bourbon. The man on the far right is dumping in some of the mash, which is being stirred by the other three men with their mash sticks, watched over by the well-dressed man by the window (perhaps S. C. Herbst). (Courtesy of Kentucky Historical Society.)

ON THE COVER: These men at the O.F.C. Distillery in Frankfort, like all the distillery crews pictured in this book, look like they are proud of their craft. The art of making whiskey has changed some over the centuries, but the most important ingredient remains the human element. No two brands of bourbon whiskey taste exactly the same because, like great chefs, master distillers can take basically the same ingredients and create something new. (Courtesy of Kentucky Historical Society.)

IMAGES
of America

THE KENTUCKY
BOURBON TRAIL

Berkeley and Jeanine Scott

ARCADIA
PUBLISHING

Copyright © 2009 by Berkeley and Jeanine Scott
ISBN 978-0-7385-6626-9

Published by Arcadia Publishing
Charleston SC, Chicago IL, Portsmouth NH, San Francisco CA

Printed in the United States of America

Library of Congress Control Number: 2009927248

For all general information contact Arcadia Publishing at:
Telephone 843-853-2070
Fax 843-853-0044
E-mail sales@arcadiapublishing.com
For customer service and orders:
Toll-Free 1-888-313-2665

Visit us on the Internet at www.arcadiapublishing.com

*We would like to dedicate this book to our loving family,
especially sons Sean and Robert, daughter-in-law Rebecca,
grandson Noah, granddaughter Alison,
and family patriarch Al Luciana and his wife, Pat.*

CONTENTS

ACKNOWLEDGMENTS

Compiling a book of historical photographs is a project that requires cooperation from a lot of people, especially this book, since it includes images provided by all eight distilleries on the Kentucky Bourbon Trail. That said, everyone we worked with was very helpful and cooperative, which made our job much easier. We would like to thank Eric Gregory and Kristin Meadors at the Kentucky Distillers' Association and all the people we worked with at the Kentucky Bourbon Trail distilleries, including Angela Traver, Al Young, Larry Kass, Joshua Hafer, Kathleen DiBenedetto, Honi Goldman, Katrina Egbert, Joseph Uranga, Chris Morris, Tracy Frederick, Svend Jansen, and Pam Gover.

More than 40 of the images in the book are from the collections at the Kentucky Historical Society. We would like to encourage all Kentuckians who have family materials that might be of interest to researchers in the future to consider donating the material to the Kentucky Historical Society. Thanks to KHS executive director Kent Whitworth, Charlene Smith, Kevin Johnson, Diane Bundy, and all the rest of the helpful staff people in the special collections and library areas at the Kentucky Historical Society.

Other museums and libraries provided materials, and we would like to thank Russ Hatter at the Capital City Museum, Mary Ellyn Hamilton at the Oscar Getz Museum of Whiskey History, Nancy Smith at the Hopewell Museum, and the staff at the Daviess County Library's Kentucky Room.

We also received material and information from Dixie Hibbs, Jeri Miller White, Bill Rodgers, Olivia Ripy, and Barry McNees. Again, thanks to everyone for their help.

Kentucky Bourbon Trail® is a registered trademark of the Kentucky Distillers' Association, and the mark and associated logos are being used by Arcadia Publishing, Inc., with its permission. The KDA and its member distilleries ask that you please enjoy Kentucky bourbon responsibly.

INTRODUCTION

Bourbon whiskey is many things to many people—a family business, an ingredient in mint juleps, Kentucky's signature industry. As this book shows, it is also part of the historical fabric of Kentucky and a traditional industry that survives and even flourishes in the present.

There have been numerous agricultural-based industries in Kentucky, such as the production of bluegrass seeds and hemp, that were dominant for a while but eventually died out. Whiskey-making certainly had to overcome multiple setbacks, including Prohibition, the Great Depression, and an embargo on whiskey production during both World Wars. That doesn't even count the many ups and downs of the business that don't deserve capital letters—droughts that literally dried up the crops needed to make bourbon whiskey and devastating fires that could wipe out years of production in the blink of an eye.

But through it all, members of distilling families kept their yeast strains alive and perfected their formulas for making what they consider the best-tasting bourbon whiskey and passed those time-honored traditions down from father to son for generations. This book contains numerous photographs of members of longtime Kentucky distilling families like the Beams, Samuelses, Ripys, Medleys, and Browns as well as other individuals who had a major impact on the industry, like the Reverend Elijah Craig and Col. E. H. Taylor Jr.

There are many other families and individuals who aren't pictured here for one reason or another. There do not seem to be any images left of Dr. James Crow, a man who developed some of the techniques pivotal to the long-term success of the bourbon whiskey industry, including possibly the method of making "sour mash" bourbon.

That Dr. Crow developed the technique of making "sour mash" bourbon would probably be disputed by descendants of several of the venerable Kentucky bourbon-making families, including the Beam family. They trace the beginning of "simon pure, old-fashioned Sour Mash Bourbon" to 1795, when Jacob Beam "migrated over land on horseback from Maryland to Nelson County, Kentucky with a small pot still on his back and began to make whiskey by the 'old-fashioned Sour Mash' whiskey-making method," according to an early booklet.

The booklet goes on to explain the labor-intensive process by which the distillers of the past and the present ensure the quality of their product. The process begins with the selection of the very best grains for the distilling and fermenting processes and doesn't end until years later, when the bourbon whiskey has undergone its transformation from the harsh "white dog" that comes out of the continuous or pot still into the mellower, amber-colored bourbon whiskey ready to be bottled. Notice the phrase "years later"—bourbon distilling is not for the impatient as, by law, bourbon has to be aged at least two years, but most is aged much longer.

Straight bourbon has to be aged at least two years because of a law passed by Congress in 1964 recognizing bourbon as "America's only native spirit." In order to be called bourbon, it must be "made with a minimum of 51 percent corn and aged for at least two years in new oak barrels that have been charred."

Bourbon can be made in other states, but Kentucky has not only the tradition of fine bourbon-making, but also the perfect climate conditions and natural resources needed for excelling at the production of bourbon. In 2007, a full 95 percent of the world's bourbon was made in Kentucky, according to the Kentucky Distillers' Association.

As to the age-old question of how bourbon was named, this book examines several of the theories, some quoted in books and articles that include the "fact" that one cannot buy bourbon in Bourbon County, which is false, as Bourbon County is not a dry county. One theory not included elsewhere was advanced by noted Kentucky historian George Chinn, who explained his theory in a 1977 article in the *Lexington Herald-Leader* in response to a book claiming that the mint julep originated in Virginia.

Chinn said that bourbon is the essential ingredient for juleps and added, "I would like to know how any other state can claim the origin of bourbon whiskey when we are the only state that has a Bourbon County, and it is a settled fact that it (bourbon) originated there."

Chinn went on to advance yet another idea about how bourbon first came to lose the clear color associated with earlier whiskeys. "What used to be called 'red liquor' or 'red whiskey' was discovered on Stoner Creek, in Bourbon County," he said. "Someone discovered that you could have charcoal in a barrel and pour whiskey on it and let it age and the chemical reaction would set up a tannic acid that made the white whiskey turn red."

Whether that is true or not, one Bourbon County man has long been linked with the craft. Jacob Spears has been credited as being one of the first bourbon distillers, and his stone house, warehouse, and springhouse are still standing in Bourbon County more than 200 years later.

Jeremiah Beam gave Spears credit in a speech he made in 1967 to the Iroquois Hunt Club in Lexington, Kentucky, as the "favorite nominee around Bourbon County" for the honor of being the first to distill bourbon. Beam quoted a contemporary of Spears who said of Spears's product, "A man can run, shoot and jump better after one drink of that noble fluid."

Bourbon is no longer made in the county that gave the amber-colored whiskey its name. Prohibition closed down the numerous large and small distilleries in the county, and when its repeal finally came along almost 14 years later, none reopened. That sad fact held true throughout the state, and the number of distilleries in the state dropped from a high point estimated in the hundreds to only about a dozen today.

This is not to say that there is less bourbon being made today than in those free-wheeling days before Prohibition. In 2007, there were 937,865 barrels of bourbon produced in the state compared with 455,078 barrels produced in 1999, and there are more than 5 million barrels of bourbon and other whiskeys currently aging in Kentucky, according to statistics compiled by the Kentucky Distillers' Association (KDA).

The year 1999 was chosen because that was the year the KDA formed the Kentucky Bourbon Trail®, which has become one of the state's best-known attractions, visited by an ever-growing number of tourists each year from all 50 states and at least 40 foreign countries.

The Kentucky Bourbon Trail allows visitors to get a behind-the-scenes look at the state's signature industry at eight well-known distilleries, and there are numerous photographs in this book from each of those distilleries. In addition, there are several other chapters filled with historical photographs of other distilleries from the past and a step-by-step photographic outline of the bourbon-distilling process. All of this material will give readers an appreciation of the time-honored and traditional craft of making bourbon—from large batch to small batch to single barrel—for the entire world to enjoy.

One

BORN IN THE BLUEGRASS

IT BEGAN WITH THE CORN. The unique taste of bourbon whiskey began with the predominance of corn as an agricultural crop in early Kentucky. Making whiskey was nothing new to many of the first pioneers who settled in the state. The difference in the whiskey they made in Kentucky compared to what they had been distilling was that corn now made up the bulk of the mash. (Courtesy of Kentucky Historical Society.)

CABIN AND CORN PATCH. Even though this photograph was taken much later, it illustrates what the early Kentucky settlers had to do in order to get title to the land. At that point, Kentucky was a part of Virginia, and Virginia law specified that settlers had to build a log cabin and plant a required number of acres of corn in order to get the all-important deed. (Courtesy of Kentucky Historical Society.)

GRAIN-HUNGRY DISTILLERIES. These men and their animals are transporting corn the old-fashioned way. The corn usually had to be transported to mills to be ground before it could be used in whiskey production by the early farmer-distillers. As distilling operations became larger, neighboring farmers could sell their excess corn crop to the closest distillery instead of having to make it into whiskey themselves. (Courtesy of Capital City Museum.)

COOL, CLEAR WATER. Although the types of grain that are mashed and fermented are an important contributor to the taste of the final product, whiskey-making also requires lots of water. The water used by Kentucky distillers differed from what was used in other areas of the country, as it had been naturally filtered through the layers of limestone that lie above and below the state's soil. (Courtesy of Kentucky Historical Society.)

GRINDING THE GRAINS. Water-driven gristmills much like the one pictured here ground grains used in various products, including whiskey. Cornmeal was a food staple on the frontier, but, financially, the best way to use corn was to distill it into whiskey, which could be sold or traded. In addition, a barrel of whiskey was much easier to transport than numerous bushels of corn. (Courtesy of Kentucky Historical Society.)

11

ON TO MAYSVILLE. The next step in the evolution of the bourbon whiskey-making industry started at the farm distilleries when more whiskey was produced than could be used or sold locally. Enterprising distillers started shipping barrels of their product down the Ohio River through the nearby port of Maysville. The town was then part of "Old Bourbon County," leading to the theory that barrels shipped from Maysville would have been marked "Old Bourbon." The people on the other end of the shipments, who recognized a quality product, started calling it bourbon, which explains how corn-based whiskey became known as bourbon whiskey. Another way the Ohio River might have influenced the whiskey is that when the Falls of the Ohio near Louisville could not be traversed, cargo was off-loaded and transported to the other side of the falls. Occasionally, it was stored until another boat was available, and as the barrels sat, the contents matured from the harsh, new whiskey available locally to something a bit more mellow. This photograph shows Maysville and the Ohio River. (Courtesy of Kentucky Historical Society.)

BIGGER AND BETTER. Steamboats like the *Courier*, shown here tied up to the wharf in Maysville, replaced the earlier, smaller boats used on the Ohio River. The bigger boats gave the distillers the ability to ship much larger numbers of barrels. That led to the concentration of the whiskey-distilling business and to larger, more industrialized distilleries that utilized more grain and produced more whiskey. (Courtesy of Kentucky Historical Society.)

BOURBON COUNTY DISTILLERS. Another theory on how bourbon whiskey got its now-famous name is that someone living in Bourbon County was the first to make what is now recognized as bourbon. Two of the people mentioned as possibly the first to make bourbon are Daniel Shawhan and Jacob Spears. Both men lived and made whiskey in Bourbon County in the 1780s. This label is from "Old Shawhan— the PIONEER Kentucky Whiskey." (Authors' collection.)

86 PROOF

THIS WHISKEY IS 4 YEARS OLD

Old Shawhan

Kentucky Straight Bourbon Whiskey

The PIONEER Kentucky Whiskey

BOTTLED BY DARLING DISTILLERY CO., SHIVELY, JEFFERSON COUNTY, KENTUCKY

BAPTIST PREACHER AND DISTILLER. Another candidate for the title of "Father of Bourbon" is the Reverend Elijah Craig. Reverend Craig was a Baptist minister who moved to Kentucky in search of religious freedom in 1781. He settled in Scott County and opened a distillery in the late 1780s. Some credit him with the discovery of the fact that charred barrels impart a smoother taste and attractive color to whiskey. (Courtesy of Heaven Hill Distilleries, Inc.)

INNOVATIVE FARMER AND DISTILLER. Jacob Spears moved to Bourbon County, Kentucky, from Pennsylvania in the 1780s and is credited with being one of the first to distill a new type of corn-based whiskey named for his home county. Spears's home, named Stone Castle, and the adjoining stone bourbon warehouse and stone springhouse are still standing today—the most complete early distiller's complex still in existence. (Courtesy of Charles S. Spears Jr.)

Two

THE ART AND SCIENCE OF BOURBON MAKING

THE SCIENCE. Distilling has always been considered both a science and, to any true lover of the "spirit world," an art form. The chemical reactions that bring on fermentation and distillation have been known for a very long time. Dr. James Crow is credited with bringing "the scientific approach" to Kentucky distilling in the mid-1800s. The chemists pictured are adding malt to a glass beaker at Frankfort's Stagg Distillery in 1940. (Courtesy of Kentucky Historical Society.)

KENTUCKY'S GOLD. Bourbon has been called "the best thing that ever happened to corn," and since corn is the predominant ingredient in the grain mixture known as the "mashbill" that bourbon whiskey is made from, it is probably true. Corn is a product of the New World, as is bourbon, and was the Kentucky pioneer's favorite crop. It contributes a lot of starch, which is converted to alcohol, and taste to the finished product. Most of the crop for today's bourbon industry comes from Kentucky and neighboring Indiana and Illinois. Today's bourbon is derived from a grain mixture that is between 51 percent and 86 percent corn, with rye, barley, and sometimes wheat making up the difference. (Courtesy of Kentucky Historical Society.)

GRAIN ELEVATOR. Corn was Kentucky's leading crop from the beginning and remained that way until burley tobacco overtook it after World War I. Kentucky and nearby states enjoy nearly the perfect climate for growing the corn needed for bourbon making. The men shown here are storing corn in a silo attached to a distillery in Bourbon County, Kentucky, sometime in the 1890s. (Authors' collection.)

MILLING THE GRAIN. This combination grain dryer and mill ground the corn and other grains in the recipe of Bardstown's Old Barton Distillers sometime in the late 1930s. Today's typical grain mixture, or mashbill, varies in proportions from brand to brand. That variation accounts for much of the difference in taste between bourbons. (Courtesy of Oscar Getz Museum of Whiskey History.)

GOOD WATER IS ESSENTIAL. The water used by bourbon distillers is naturally filtered through the layers of limestone that lay beneath Central Kentucky. The water is iron-free and rich in magnesium and calcium, making it among the sweetest in the world. This hard water combination of minerals also makes the enzymes produced during mashing more efficient. An abundant and consistent supply of water is necessary for any distiller. (Courtesy of Kentucky Historical Society.)

OLD TAYLOR MASH TUBS. These 11,000-gallon carbon-steel mash tubs were installed in the Old Crow and Old Taylor Distillery in Woodford County in 1936. They were designed to cook the water and mash to a temperature of 212–214 degrees before the mixture was cooled and then pumped into the fermentation tubs. (Courtesy of Kentucky Historical Society.)

FILLING MASH TUBS. Father and son master distillers, Parker (left) and Earl Beam keep close watch as the combination of cooled mash, yeast, and backset (sour mash) is added to the huge cypress wood vats at Heaven Hill Distilleries in Bardstown. The mixture ferments for about three days, during which time it will bubble and smell of oatmeal and beer. (Courtesy of Heaven Hill Distilleries, Inc.)

FERMENTATION TUBS. These giant cypress tubs, pictured in 1940, began the fermentation/distillation process at the Old Joe Distillery at Bonds Mill in Anderson County for many years. "Old Joe" referred to Joe Payton, an early Kentucky settler and distiller. The plant was also known as Old Prentice and is now home to Four Roses. (Courtesy of Kentucky Historical Society.)

DISTILLATION BEGINS. After fermenting in the mash tubs, the mixture is called "distiller's beer" and is pumped into the steam-heated distilling units. This 1935 photograph shows a large metal mash drop tub and doubler that distills the mixture a second time. Since alcohol boils at a lower temperature than water, the alcohol separates from the "beer" and rises up the tubes of the still in the form of steam. (Courtesy of Kentucky Historical Society.)

Continuous or Column Still. The original continuous still was patented in Britain in 1831. It took hold in America during the Industrial Revolution, and most American distillers use a modern variation today. A continuous still sustains a constant process of distillation, while a pot still can only work one batch at a time. The tall column still seen in this 1890s photograph was at the Old Fire Copper (O.F.C.) Distillery in Frankfort. One young man (peering into the cup) seems to be stirring a mash tub with a wooden paddle. More modern tubs have powered stirrers to do this backbreaking job. O.F.C. eventually became today's Buffalo Trace. (Courtesy of Buffalo Trace Distillery.)

LAST POT STILL. Pictured is the last copper pot still, also known as a "batch still," used by Medley Distillery in Owensboro after the company changed over to the more efficient column or continuous stills. Most of Kentucky's bourbon makers now use continuous stills except Maker's Mark and Woodford Reserve, which had three large copper pot stills made in Scotland to triple-distill their whiskey. (Courtesy of Kentucky Room/Daviess County Public Library.)

TAIL BOX HOLDS "WHITE DOG." When the distilling process is done, the crystal clear "high wine," or "white dog," passes through a copper and glass "spirit safe," or "tail box," so that a highly experienced stillman can check with his eyes and nose for the desired quality. This new liquid is anywhere between 120 and 140 proof. The men pictured here are at Frankfort's George T. Stagg Distillery in 1940. (Courtesy of Kentucky Historical Society.)

CHARRING BARRELS. New barrels of American white oak are formed at cooperages like Brown-Forman's Bluegrass Cooperage in Louisville. They weigh about 100 pounds empty and about 500 pounds full. The caramelized flavor of the char and wood "marry" with the stored whiskey to give bourbon its wonderfully distinct flavor. (Courtesy of Brown-Forman Corporation.)

FILLING BARRELS. Federal standards require that the bourbon going into the barrels cannot be more than 125 proof. Since some bourbon makers distill at a higher proof, water may be added to the barrel to meet this requirement. These officials at the Old Crow and Old Taylor Distillery in Millville near Frankfort are gauging, filling, and weighing the barrels before they are stored for their "long nap." (Courtesy of Jeri Miller White.)

SEALING BARRELS. Leon Thornberry at the J. T. S. Brown and Son Distillery is pounding in the poplar bung, sealing the barrel before it goes to the warehouse. This distillery was located with others on the Kentucky River in the town of Tyrone. Once a bustling distilling center that shipped its product by riverboat, Tyrone is now nearly abandoned. (Courtesy of Ripy Family Collection.)

LABELING BARRELS. Before barrels are stored away in warehouses (rickhouses) for anywhere from two to 20 years, they must be properly dated, numbered, and labeled, as J. T. S. Brown workers Mike Adams (left) and Jim McGinnes are doing in Anderson County. Most warehouses are six to nine stories high, although a few are just one, with barrels stacked three high on wooden racks called "ricks." (Courtesy of Ripy Family Collection.)

An Inside Look. A tornado that roared through Lawrenceburg and the J. T. S. Brown Distillery in 1965 provided this cutaway look inside a bourbon barrel warehouse. The barrels are stored in racks (ricks) usually three high that are designed for good air circulation. Many of the warehouses that dot Central Kentucky are six to nine stories high and contain as many as 20,000 barrels. Each distiller has different requirements for their warehouses: some want them on top of hills, some in valleys. Some rickhouses are heated, and some are not temperature controlled at all. In the latter category, some distillers may rotate their barrels as the bourbon ages, while some prefer to blend the whiskey from the warmer top floors with a barrel from the cooler floors below to achieve a consistent product. (Courtesy of Ripy Family Collection.)

AGING BOURBON. For a whiskey to be called straight bourbon, it must be aged in new, charred oak barrels for at least two years, but most are aged at least four and some as long as 20 years. The men in this 1935 picture have rolled the barrels down the center aisle and are lifting the barrels into the ricks of the old Labrot and Graham Distillery in Woodford County. (Courtesy of Kentucky Historical Society.)

SAMPLING WITH WHISKEY THIEF. As the bourbon ages over the years, master distillers like Elmer T. Lee at Buffalo Trace (left) will use a "whiskey thief" to sample the whiskey as it matures and takes on the distinctive flavors and other characteristics that the charred oak barrels provide. Lee is assisted by Obie Kemper. (Courtesy of Buffalo Trace Distillery.)

Filling Sacks with Produlac. One of the by-products of bourbon making is "spent beer," the wet, mushy sludge that is left after the first distillation. Some is put aside to provide the "setback" that creates the sour mash; the rest is often dried and sold as cattle feed. This picture shows men bagging the dried feed that was marketed under the name Produlac by National Distillers in 1939. (Courtesy of Kentucky Historical Society.)

Filtering Bourbon. When the presiding master distiller determines that the whiskey has slumbered enough and is ready for bottling, it is emptied from the barrels (as seen here) and filtered, removing harmless impurities that might cloud the beautiful amber liquid in the bottle. Some believe that filtering takes away a little flavor, so some premium "heritage" brands are unfiltered. (Courtesy of Buffalo Trace Distillery.)

BOTTLES AND CASES OF OLD JUDGE. In the early years of whiskey-making, customers bought their bourbon directly from the barrel, carrying away their purchase in jugs or quart jars. As glass bottles became more available toward the end of the 1890s, brands like Old Judge packaged their product in the more convenient and attractive containers. (Courtesy of Kentucky Historical Society.)

ALL IN ONE ROOM. This 1898 photograph shows the Old Taylor bottling line. The bottles are filled from the large metal tank in the corner and then capped, labeled, and sealed. The bottles then go in cases, which move along the conveyor belt that the man in the background is leaning on, out the door, and into a waiting railcar or wagon. (Courtesy of Kentucky Historical Society.)

Three

FASCINATING PEOPLE AND PLACES

A DAY AT COON HOLLOW. Richard Cummins and his brother Patrick were both trained as yeast makers and distillers and moved to America from Ireland in 1848. Richard worked with Henry McKenna until after the Civil War, when he set up his own distillery in Nelson County and called it Coon Hollow. Richard Cummins is pictured here (second from left on platform) with some of his workmen in 1890. (Courtesy of Oscar Getz Museum of Whiskey History.)

MASSIVE WAREHOUSE. This oversized bourbon warehouse has eight floors, and the size dwarfs the men standing in the doorway of the building behind the line of barrels. This photograph was probably taken at Forks of Elkhorn, where the north and south forks of Elkhorn Creek meet before running into the Kentucky River near Frankfort. That distillery was run by W. J. Baker after the Civil War, and they produced the Old Baker and Old Cabinet brands. The two well-dressed men in the foreground are possibly Baker and his son. (Courtesy of Kentucky Historical Society.)

Way Up There. This photograph shows a large, brick distillery building under construction, probably in the Frankfort area. At the top of the very tall brick chimney are three workmen, and two additional men can be seen lower down on the roof. The quality of construction and the materials used varied widely among distilleries, and this brick building was certainly on the high end of the spectrum. The problem with sinking a lot of money into high-end buildings was that there was always the possibility of some disaster lurking around the corner—like Prohibition. (Courtesy of Kentucky Historical Society.)

FROM "WHISKEY ROUTE" TO WHISKEY DISTILLERY. According to Sam Cecil's *The Evolution of the Bourbon Whiskey Industry in Kentucky*, the Old Kennebec Distillery was built in the late 1930s by J. M. Perkins, who was a Frankfort banker and the owner of the Frankfort and Cincinnati Railroad. The F&C was called the "Whiskey Route" because it served many of the distilleries along its route between Paris and Frankfort. (Courtesy of Capital City Museum.)

HEADED FOR TEXAS. This photograph shows a railroad car full of Cedar Run whiskey parked on a railroad siding in Frankfort. The Cedar Run Distillery was run by J. and J. M. Saffell. A note in the 1889 *Wine and Spirits Bulletin* stated that "Messers. J. and J. M. Saffell of Frankfort will make but a limited supply of their well-known brand 'Cedar Run' this season." (Courtesy of Kentucky Historical Society.)

A Busy Place. There's no question about which distillery is pictured here—the John E. Fitzgerald Company believed in signage. The distillery was located on Benson Creek outside Frankfort. It produced Old Fitzgerald, Old Judge, and Benson Springs. S. C. Herbst was the distributor of the whiskey until Fitzgerald sold the distillery to Herbst around 1900. Herbst can be seen in several of the other photographs of the distillery, including the first photograph in this book. It is possible that he can also be seen seated in the buggy in the center of this photograph. (Courtesy of Kentucky Historical Society.)

FAMOUS OLD CROW SPRING. This 1880s photograph was taken of two dapper gentlemen with their canine friend at the spring at the Old Crow Distillery on Glenn's Creek. Old Crow was named for Dr. James Crow, who used his scientific expertise to improve the consistency of whiskey distilling by inventing the "sour mash" technique, which uses a small amount of the previous batch in the current batch. (Courtesy of Kentucky Historical Society.)

LABELING OLD CROW. These ladies are putting labels and tax stamps on bottles of Old Crow produced by the W. A. Gaines Company. Once whiskey began being sold in bottles instead of barrels, women were able to move into the distillery workforce. The tax stamps showed that the whiskey was "bottled in bond," which was a guarantee of its quality. (Courtesy of Kentucky Historical Society.)

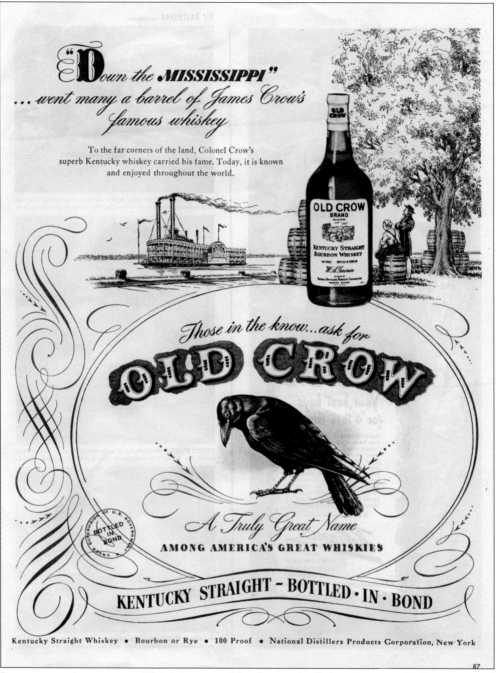

IMAGINATIVE ADVERTISING. This is just one of the thousands of advertisements that have appeared touting a particular kind of whiskey as the best ever. The first known bourbon advertisement was printed in the *Western Citizen* in Paris, Kentucky, in 1821. One thing to notice in this advertisement is that Dr. James Crow is now a colonel. The Old Crow Distillery continued to produce bourbon under the ownership of National Distillers until the 1980s, when it was purchased by the Jim Beam Brands Company. Although the distillery on Glenn's Creek is no longer active, the facility is still used by the Jim Beam Brands Company to store bourbon. (Authors' collection.)

Man's Best Friends. A group including Kenner Taylor, one of Col. E. H. Taylor Jr.'s sons, purchased what remained of the Baker Distillery at the Forks of Elkhorn in 1933. Their brands included Kenner Taylor, Golden Bantam, and Forks of Elkhorn. Unfortunately, the back of this postcard is missing, so the story of the two white dogs pictured in the lower corner can no longer be told. (Courtesy of Capital City Museum.)

It Takes Two. National Distillers purchased the K. Taylor plant, renovated and expanded it, and operated it as Old Grand-Dad. The brands Old Taylor and Old Crow were also owned by National Distillers at this point and were also produced and bottled at the Old Grand-Dad Distillery. The two ladies in the photograph are identified as "National Distiller's stamp machine girls." (Courtesy of Kentucky Historical Society.)

CRAFTSMANSHIP

One of the prime elements of good craftsmanship is pleasure in the doing. Certainly this is true of Old Grand-Dad. For when you take your first sip of this fine bonded bourbon you just naturally feel that he who made it took great delight in his craft. And that out of this delight he imparted to Old Grand-Dad a flavor, aroma and mellowness such as you've not experienced in many a long day. Why not make that long day a short one hereafter by taking Old Grand-Dad permanently into your family circle?

OLD GRAND-DAD

Bottled in Bond — 100 Proof

Head of the Bourbon Family

NATIONAL DISTILLERS PRODUCTS CORPORATION, NEW YORK

HEAD OF THE FAMILY. According to this advertisement, Old Grand-Dad is the "Head of the Bourbon Family." The brand began in the 1880s and has been produced at several distilleries, including the one named after it in Frankfort. The bust being carved in the advertisement is of Basil Hayden, the originator of the recipe for Old Grand-Dad, which contains more rye than many bourbon whiskeys. The company that first made Old Grand-Dad was founded by R. B. Hayden, and he named the brand after his grandfather, Basil Hayden Sr., a well-known distiller during his lifetime. The brand's label used a drawing of Basil Hayden Sr. until 1939, when National Distillers, who owned the brand at that time, commissioned the bust of the famous grandfather that can be seen in this advertisement. Today Old Grand-Dad is a Jim Beam brand. (Authors' collection.)

HIS HONOR THE MAYOR. Col. E. H. Taylor Jr. knew something about politics as well as distilling premium whiskey. Colonel Taylor was orphaned as a young boy and lived for several years with his great-uncle Zachary Taylor in New Orleans before he was elected president of the United States. After moving back to Frankfort as an adult, Colonel Taylor was elected to several terms as mayor. (Courtesy of Kentucky Historical Society.)

LOVELY HOME. Thistleton is the name of this attractive home where Colonel Taylor lived later in his life. He was also a well-known breeder of Hereford cattle. Colonel Taylor was best known, however, as a distiller and was involved in the distilling business from 1865 until he died at the age of 92 in 1922 having been either owner or manager of six different distilleries. (Courtesy of Kentucky Historical Society.)

UNDER CONSTRUCTION. This photograph is labeled "group working at E. H. Taylor Distilling—Thistleton." The building under construction in the background looks like it might be a barn. Some of the carpenters and workmen are wearing aprons emblazoned with the names of several Frankfort businesses, including Hammond and Company Lumber. (Courtesy of Kentucky Historical Society.)

FANCY BOTTLING ROOM. This bottling room at the E. H. Taylor and Sons Distillery on Glenn's Creek outside of Frankfort was a thing of beauty. Colonel Taylor was a perfectionist who believed in doing everything first-class and was among the first to welcome tours and public events at his distillery. In this room, Old Taylor whiskey was "bottled-in-bond" under government supervision and sealed with the familiar green revenue stamp. (Courtesy of Kentucky Historical Society.)

A GRAND OLD TIME. It looks like everyone in this photograph, taken around 1900 at the Old Taylor Distillery, is having a great time. The distillery was the site of many celebrations and events like this Elk's Club reunion. Not only did Colonel Taylor build a castle-like distillery, he surrounded it with sunken gardens and other visitor-friendly improvements. Unfortunately, the distillery site is now abandoned. (Courtesy of Kentucky Historical Society.)

SPRING BEAUTY. Colonel Taylor also designed an art-noveau-style springhouse with carved limestone columns with Ionic capitals surrounding the spring that was the distillery's water supply. The reservoir area was built in the shape of a keyhole, indicating that the water the spring produced was the key to the success of the bourbon produced there. The men pictured are from National Distillers, which purchased the distillery in 1935. (Courtesy of Jere Miller White.)

CART FULL OF BOURBON. Whether O.F.C. stood for Old Fire Copper or Old Fashioned Copper when these two men were transporting a cart-load of cases of it isn't really important. Col. E. H. Taylor Jr. first produced O.F.C. Whiskey, but it was one of the brands that he lost to George T. Stagg when Taylor encountered economic difficulties and Stagg took over the distilleries Taylor had built. (Courtesy of Capital City Museum.)

OLD FASHIONED COPPER LABEL. When Col. E. H. Taylor named his magnificent new distillery on the banks of the Kentucky River O.F.C. in 1870, he meant "Old Fire Copper." This let people know that the whiskey was distilled in all-copper equipment, which was supposed to be cleaner. Perhaps later owners felt that possible consumers were no longer familiar with the term and began labeling it "Old Fashioned Copper." (Courtesy of Kentucky Historical Society.)

Room Full of Stags. There are several stags pictured around this office at the George Stagg Distillery, which is now Buffalo Trace. It is possible that the man seated at the desk is George T. Stagg. Stagg was Colonel Taylor's partner until money problems forced Taylor out of the partnership. Taylor then formed the company E. H. Taylor and Sons and built the Old Taylor Distillery on Glenn's Creek. (Courtesy of Bill Rodgers Collection.)

Nice Layout. From the cars that can be seen, it looks like this photograph was taken in the 1920s or 1930s. The George T. Stagg Distillery continued to produce whiskey for medicinal purposes during the lean years of Prohibition, which made it easier to start up regular production once Prohibition was over. The photograph shows the distillery complex surrounded on three sides by undeveloped land. (Courtesy of Capital City Museum.)

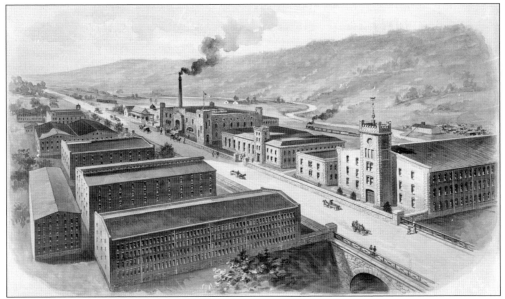

OUT OF SCALE. This detailed painting of the Old Taylor Distillery on Glenn's Creek outside of Frankfort is filled with information about the distillery operation, but the one drawback is that it is not in scale—the people and carriages shown are tiny compared to the two- and three-story distillery buildings. Notice the distinctive springhouse on the left. (Courtesy of Kentucky Historical Society.)

DOOR-TO-DOOR SERVICE. As can be seen in several of the distillery photographs, railroad tracks ran very close to the buildings, making it easy for workmen to load cases of bourbon into the boxcars. The cases are labeled E. H. Taylor and Sons and Old Taylor. The posters on the wall are for a fair in Sanders, Kentucky, in what looks like September 1910. (Courtesy of Kentucky Historical Society.)

WAITING FOR THE TRAIN. The railroads provided an important transportation link between the distilleries, many in semi-rural or rural areas, and the liquor distributors across the country. This photograph of a freight depot includes many cases of bottles of Old Taylor, Old Crow, and Old Hermitage bourbon in the outgoing freight waiting for the next train. In addition, on the end of the freight cart in the center, there is a bourbon barrel harking back to the older methods of transporting whiskey. Colonel Taylor worked hard for passage of the Bottled-in-Bond Act of 1897, which set out guidelines for labeling and bottling bourbon whiskey. Up to that point, whiskey was sold in barrels and distillers had no control over what happened to the bourbon after they sold it to the distributors but before it reached the consumers. Some distributors added water and flavorings to increase their profits, so consistency became a problem. (Courtesy of Kentucky Historical Society.)

"Ding" Went the Trolley. This interesting photograph shows the office at what is now Buffalo Trace Distillery divided up between "E. H. Taylor, Jr. Co. Incorporated, Distiller" and "Geo. T. Stagg Co. Incorporated, Wholesale Liquor Dealer." Stagg was a liquor distributor before he met Colonel Taylor and became his partner. From the signage, it appears he continued in that business after the partnership was formed as well. The trolley driver looks like he just stopped long enough to have his photograph taken. (Courtesy of Bill Rodgers Collection.)

AERIAL VIEW. This photograph shows the Old Hermitage Distillery on the Kentucky River in Frankfort. On the top of the bluff on the other side of the river is the Frankfort Cemetery. The distillery was built in 1868 by the firm of Gaines, Berry, and Company and acquired by National Distillers in 1929. It has been suggested that the brand name came from the name of Andrew Jackson's home in Tennessee. (Courtesy of Capital City Museum.)

WHISKEY RODE THE RAILS. The Old '76 distillery was near the Licking River and right next to the railroad tracks south of Newport in Campbell County in Northern Kentucky. It produced Medallion Sour Mash Whiskey and Woodruff "Double Distilled" whiskey from 1904 until it closed in 1918. It never reopened after Prohibition ended. (Courtesy of Kentucky Historical Society.)

STONE DISTILLERY ON KENTUCKY RIVER. One of the most attractive small distilleries in Kentucky was the E. J. Curly Distillery, built of limestone on the banks of the Kentucky River at Camp Nelson in Jessamine County. Built in 1880, the distillery's brands included Boone's Knoll, Royal Bourbon, and Blue Grass Bourbon. The operation almost crashed in 1889, when the owner had his horses and wagons impounded for tax delinquency. In 1923, during Prohibition, it was converted into a hotel with beautiful views of the river and palisades. After Prohibition, it returned as Kentucky River Distillery and operated into the 1970s, adding the Old Lazy Days brand to its list. Some of the operation's warehouses can be seen back in the trees. (Courtesy of Oscar Getz Museum of Whiskey History.)

OLD DARLING BALL CLUB. In 1911, when this photograph was taken, many of Kentucky's distilleries sponsored baseball teams. Possibly the only distillery ever in Carroll County, it began as Whitehead and Company in Prestonville sometime before 1879. It was bought in 1880 by Andrew Darling, who created the brands Old Darling, Carroll County Club Bourbon, and Carroll County Rye. Notice the natty batboy with his bare feet. (Courtesy of Kentucky Historical Society.)

BOURBON GOING UP OR DOWN RIVER. Riverboats on the Ohio River were still an important way to transport goods around 1900, when this photograph was taken in Carrolton of barrels of Old Darling Bourbon being loaded on this Cincinnati-based boat. Eventually the railroad and modern trucks sank the riverboat industry. (Courtesy of Oscar Getz Museum of Whiskey History.)

A "MEDLEY" OF GOOD WISHES

FOR A JOYOUS HOLIDAY AND A
HAPPY, PROSPEROUS NEW YEAR

A good wish—like good whiskey—can be taken straight! So . . . Here's to you! "MERRY CHRISTMAS"—straight from the heart! The whole Medley family joins in the chorus, wishing you a barrel of fun . . . and a spirited success in 1938!

John A. Medley   Ben F. Medley   Geo. E. Medley, II   Geo. E. Medley, III
Parker J. Medley   Ben F. Medley, II   Ed. W. Medley
Thos. A. Medley, Jr.

Owensboro Kentucky   Richard Wathen Medley

THE MEDLEY FAMILY
THREE GENERATIONS OF KNOWING HOW
THE DAVIESS COUNTY DISTILLING CO.

THOMAS A. MEDLEY
President

KENTUCKY STRAIGHT   BOURBON WHISKEY

GREETINGS FROM THE MEDLEY FAMILY. This 1937 magazine advertisement was directed to liquor distributors during a time when the Medley clan was one of Kentucky's leading distilling families. They claim an eight-generation history of making bourbon in the state, and they have been in Owensboro and Daviess County since 1878. The Medleys intermarried with another Kentucky distilling family, the Wathens, who distilled the famous Old Grand-Dad brand in their Nelson County distillery. The Daviess County Distilling Company was begun in 1873 and was purchased by George Medley in 1901. It melded into Medley Distilling Company in 1940 and finally closed in 1991. A new venture, Charles Medley Distillers Kentucky, emerged in 2009 and hopes to have aged bourbon to sell within a few years. (Courtesy of Kentucky Historical Society.)

FACILITY ON THE OHIO RIVER. This 1957 aerial photograph has been identified as either the Medley Distillery or the Glenmore Distillery in Owensboro. They were very close to each other. Glenmore Distillery was formed out of the Monarch Distillery bankruptcy in 1901 by James Thompson. In 1991, Glenmore Distillery and brands were purchased by United Distillers, and the distillery operation was moved to Louisville. (Courtesy of Kentucky Room/Daviess County Public Library.)

TWO MILLION BARRELS. This 1955 photograph commemorates the two-millionth barrel of bourbon made at the Glenmore Distillery in Owensboro. Two of the men in the photograph are identified as James E. Thompson (second from left) and Frank Englehard (far right); the other two are unidentified. The narrow-gauge railroad at Glenmore shuttled barrels around the large facility. (Courtesy of Oscar Getz Museum of Whiskey History.)

OUT FOR A STROLL. These four well-dressed ladies accompanied by a man look like they are out for a stroll on a warm day in 1900 at the J. W. M. Field Distillery near Owensboro. According to *The Evolution of the Bourbon Whiskey Industry in Kentucky* by Sam Cecil, the distillery started out in 1873 with a capacity of only 2.5 bushels per day but increased its daily capacity over the years to 250 bushels. Prohibition forced the distillery to close, and it never reopened. This was true of hundreds of distilleries across the commonwealth. The effect of Prohibition on the state's economy was devastating and wide-ranging. Not only were the people who worked at the distilleries out of a job, but it adversely affected everyone from the coal miners who mined the coal that kept the distilleries' steam engines running to the farmers who grew the hundreds of thousands of bushels of grains used every year. (Courtesy of Kentucky Historical Society.)

CHICKEN COCK DISTILLERY. Located just east of Paris, the Chicken Cock Distillery, originally White and Alexander, was built in 1856. Its most successful brands included Chicken Cock and Sweet Mash Bourbon. Besides a large brick distillery, the site also had warehouses for up to 30,000 barrels, a cooperage, a cattle barn, and grain bins. It was later used as a bluegrass seed cleaning facility and burned in 1961. (Courtesy of Hopewell Museum.)

ROLL OUT THE BARRELS. The men pictured here are either picking up or delivering barrels of Bourbon County whiskey during the 1880s. During that time, bourbon, tobacco, and bluegrass seed warehouses were scattered around Paris, and there were seven operating bourbon distilleries in the county. The last closed for good at the beginning of Prohibition. However, despite rumors to the contrary, Bourbon County is not dry. (Courtesy of Hopewell Museum.)

BOURBON COUNTY'S PEACOCK DISTILLERY. H. C. Bowen's Peacock Distillery was built just 5 miles north of Paris in Bourbon County around 1857. It changed hands a number of times, the Old Peacock brand being a popular one. The plant at its height had a mashing capacity of 600 bushels, or 50 to 60 barrels of whiskey a day, and two warehouses that could contain 12,000 barrels. In 1900, when this photograph was possibly taken, the distillery was owned by the Kessler Company of Cincinnati. The long stick-like item the two men are holding is a "barrel" or "whiskey thief," used to taste the whiskey from barrels as it is aging. The distillery was dismantled in 1916. (Courtesy of Hopewell Museum.)

BOLDRICK AND CALLAGHAN DISTILLERY. Richard Wathen operated a distillery on the Rolling Fork River in Marion County from 1852 to 1875. The facility was sold in 1880 to Ralph Spalding, who changed the name to Belle of Marion Distillery. It soon became Boldrick and Callaghan and produced whiskey right up to Prohibition. This photograph is from around 1885. (Courtesy of Oscar Getz Whiskey Museum.)

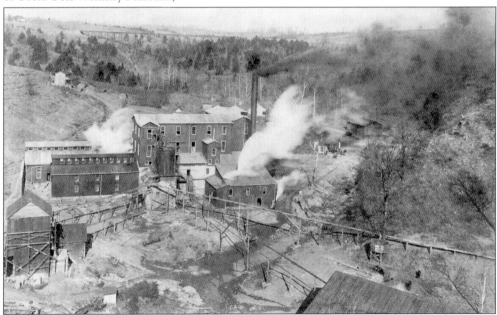

CEDAR BROOK DISTILLERY. William H. McBrayer established his distillery on Cedar Brook Run just east of Lawrenceburg in 1844. Cedar Brook whiskey won a medal at the Philadelphia Centennial in 1876. The distillery was run by his family until 1899, when it was sold to Julius Kessler and Company. In 1903, the company installed the 2.5-mile water line to the Kentucky River seen at the bottom of this picture. (Courtesy of Ripy Family Collection.)

W. F. Bond. John Bond built his distillery in 1820 near the site of the future McBrayer facility in Anderson County. His son, W. F. Bond, took over the facility in 1849 and formed a partnership with his brother-in-law, C. C. Lillard, in 1869. The distillery and name was sold to Lexington's Stoll and Company, which won the grand prize for their whiskey at the 1904 Louisiana Purchase Exposition in St. Louis. (Courtesy of Ripy Family Collection.)

John M. Atherton. In 1867, John Atherton built a distillery near the junction of Rolling Fork and Knob Creek in Larue County. He was elected as a state legislator and was chairman of the Democratic State Central Committee as well as a founding director of the Kentucky Distillers' Association. Atherton was a very successful businessman who built two other distilleries and made sizeable contributions to his alma mater, Georgetown College. (Courtesy of Dixie Hibbs.)

55

BROWN-FORMAN'S FIRST DISTILLERY. Shortly after the Civil War, J. B. Mattingly began operating the distillery shown here at St. Mary's in Marion County. Initially he had no warehouses and sold his product directly to wholesalers and saloons. In 1901, Louisville's Brown-Forman Company was formed, and they bought into Mattingly's distillery. The plant shut down in 1918 and was totally destroyed by fire in 1919. (Courtesy of Brown-Forman Corporation.)

THOMAS BEEBE RIPY. T. B. Ripy was born in 1847, son of an Irish immigrant, John Ripy, who learned whiskey distilling from his father. In 1868, John Ripy built the first distillery in Tyrone, the river town a few miles east of Lawrenceburg in Anderson County. T. B. Ripy built an additional distillery there and by the late 1890s was known as the world's largest independent sour mash distiller. (Courtesy of Ripy Family Collection.)

ERNEST W. RIPY SR. After graduating from business college in Lexington in 1896, E. W. Ripy went to work with his father, T. B. Ripy. They sold the two distilleries they owned in Tyrone to Kentucky Distilleries in 1899. In 1905, E. W. Ripy and his brothers, Ezra, Forest, and J. C. Ripy, built the Ripy Brothers Distillery. The Ripys continued to be involved with J. T. S. Brown Distilling and today's Wild Turkey brands. (Courtesy of Ripy Family Collection.)

"RIVERBOAT'S A'COMIN'!" This riverboat is about to dock around 1900 at Tyrone, a town south of Frankfort on the Kentucky River that at the time was home to a number of distilleries. The Louisville Southern railroad bridge seen in the photograph was built in 1889. The last train traveled across it in 1985. The 1,659-foot-long bridge stands 283 feet above the water. (Courtesy of Ripy Family Collection.)

BIG BUSINESS. This photograph, taken in 1936, shows the extent of the James E. Pepper Distillery on the Old Frankfort Pike near downtown Lexington after it was renovated when Prohibition ended. The fortunes of the bourbon whiskey industry rose and fell during the years after James Pepper first built the distillery in 1880. Now on the upswing, the renewed interest in bourbon has sparked a renewed interest in reusing the buildings that have not been used for distilling since the late 1960s. Current plans call for the Lexington Distillery District to utilize the James E. Pepper Distillery as well as other nearby distillery properties for redevelopment into an arts and entertainment area. In fact, plans are underway to bring bourbon distilling back to Lexington sometime in the future. Project organizers hope to produce, age, and bottle Barrel House Bourbon in the Lexington Distillery District in the next few years. (Courtesy of Messer Construction Company.)

SAMUELS FAMILY PATRIARCH. Taylor Williams (T. W.) Samuels greatly expanded the family farm and distilling operation around 1844 and introduced the family's first branded bourbon to Kentucky in the spring of 1855. T. W.'s grandfather Robert moved his family and his still to Kentucky in the spring of 1784 after mustering out of the Pennsylvania militia. (Courtesy of Maker's Mark Distillery.)

TAYLOR WILLIAM SAMUELS
FOUNDER OF T.W.SAMUELS DISTILLERY IN 1844

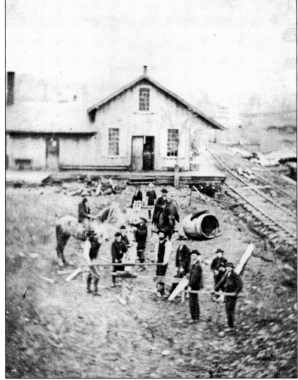

RARE PHOTOGRAPH OF OLD SAMUELS DEPOT. After T. W. Samuels built the T. W. Samuels Distillery and launched the family's bourbon-producing dynasty, each generation succeeded their fathers as proprietors until Prohibition. In 1933, T. W.'s great-grandson T. W. (Bill Sr.) helped resurrect the family distillery, anticipating Prohibition's repeal. World War II closed all of the country's distilleries and forced the sale of the Samuels distillery. A decade later, Bill Sr. started a new distillery and a new bourbon—Maker's Mark. (Courtesy of Maker's Mark Distillery.)

ENJOY THE KENTUCKY BOURBON TRAIL. Each of the next eight chapters in the book focuses on one of the distilleries on the Kentucky Bourbon Trail, which is an attraction that celebrates the heritage of Kentucky bourbon, bringing to life the people, places, and events that signify the bourbon industry. (Courtesy of Kentucky Distillers' Association.)

Four

BUFFALO TRACE

BUILT TO LAST. In 1869, Col. E. H. Taylor Jr. purchased the small distillery on the current Buffalo Trace Distillery site and invested a small fortune upgrading the facility. This photograph shows the wonderfully detailed buildings and the unusual fluted smokestacks. Taylor named the distillery O.F.C. for Old Fire Copper. The railroad car in the foreground holds coal, which powered the steam distilling process. (Courtesy of Kentucky Historical Society.)

ROLL OUT THE BARRELS. Distillery workers and government officials turned out to have their photograph taken with a group of barrels of O.F.C. bourbon. On the right is Warehouse C, built in 1885 and still in use today. In fact, the fourth and fifth floors of steam-heated Warehouse C continue to produce some of Buffalo Trace's best whiskey. (Courtesy of Kentucky Historical Society.)

A VIEW FROM ABOVE. This view shows the O.F.C. (Old Fire Copper) Distillery in all its glory on the east bank of the Kentucky River on about the same site as the pioneer settlement of Leestown just outside Frankfort. Colonel Taylor gave the distillery that name because the whiskey touched nothing but copper during the entire distilling process. (Courtesy of Kentucky Historical Society.)

QUITE A CREW. The men in an 1890s distillery crew at the E. H. Taylor Distillery are shown in front of Riverside, a stone house built in 1792 by Commodore Richard Taylor that is still part of the Buffalo Trace complex today. Most of the men are holding the tools they used every day. In the back row, two of the men are holding mashsticks that were used to stir the fermenting mash. At the far right is one man holding a mash tub, and it looks like the man on the end in the straw hat is holding a yeast jug and perhaps a thermometer. The men at far left both have shovels and what look like large pieces of coal in front of them. The next two men look like they have wrenches or some other type of hand tool. Notice the barrel in front with 10 bands (most today have six) and the backwards "Taylor" stencil. (Courtesy of Kentucky Historical Society.)

NOT EVEN A RIPPLE. The Kentucky River looks as calm as a lake in this photograph, which shows the back of what is now the Buffalo Trace Distillery and was then the O.F.C. Distillery in the background. In 1886, Colonel Taylor sold the distillery to George T. Stagg, and in 1904, the distillery was rechristened as the George T. Stagg Distillery. (Courtesy of Bill Rodgers Collection.)

ROLLING ON THE RIVER. This photograph of the Falls City steamboat going through Lock No. 4 on the Kentucky River gives another view of the distillery in the background. Some of the whiskey distilled on the site in the late 1700s was shipped down the river to New Orleans. The riverboats provided the best means of transportation for the barrels of whiskey until the railroads came along. (Courtesy of Kentucky Historical Society.)

WELL-DRESSED COLONEL. Albert Blanton was 16 when he started work at the distillery in 1897 as an office boy. He worked there for the next 50 years. By 1921, he was president of the whiskey plant. That was during Prohibition, but the distillery received a permit that allowed it to continue to make whiskey for medicinal purposes. He was named a Kentucky colonel and was usually called "Colonel Blanton." (Courtesy of Buffalo Trace Distillery.)

TRAIN STOP. The Frankfort and Cincinnati Railroad (F&C) operated between Paris and Frankfort and was known as the "Whiskey Route" because it serviced many of the distilleries in the area. This photograph shows the train making a stop at what is now Buffalo Trace Distillery to pick up a shipment of bourbon, probably in the early 1900s. The F&C was a short-line railroad that connected to the Louisville and Nashville rail lines. (Courtesy of Buffalo Trace Distillery.)

EXPANSION AFTER PROHIBITION. This photograph titled "Boiler House Addition" is dated February 23, 1937. Many distilleries went on a building spree after Prohibition was finally lifted in 1933. The year 1937 was also the year of the "Great Flood" in Frankfort that inundated the distillery. Colonel Blanton had the distillery back to normal operations within 24 hours after the Kentucky River receded. (Courtesy of Buffalo Trace Distillery.)

POSTWAR EXPANSION. By 1950, World War II was over and the Stagg Distillery began a building program that included adding Warehouse S. The elevated barrel rolling track in the foreground of this photograph holds what looks like some of the first barrels being warehoused for their mandatory aging period. All bourbon labeled as "straight Kentucky bourbon whiskey" must age at least two years in charred oak barrels, but much of it ages longer. (Courtesy of Buffalo Trace Distillery.)

WHO'S COUNTING? All distilleries make a big deal out of milestone barrels, and who can blame them? The celebrations are great occasions to show off the popularity of their whiskey. In 1951, sales of Old Stagg reached 1.2 million cases, and the next year, this barrel celebration was held. Longtime distillery manager Albert Blanton, who had led the distillery through Prohibition, the Depression, and two world wars, retired in 1951. (Courtesy of Buffalo Trace Distillery.)

World's Only One-Barrel Bonded Whiskey Warehouse

WORLD'S SMALLEST. This postcard shows Warehouse V—the world's only one-barrel bonded warehouse—built in 1952 to hold the two-millionth barrel of Old Stagg. The back of the card reads, "This barrel of Old Stagg—America's Largest Selling Kentucky Bourbon—will patiently age and mellow in this 'unique' shrine to Kentucky whiskey." The warehouse is still in use and currently holds the six-millionth barrel filled at the distillery. (Authors' collection.)

ONE OF MANY. Ancient Age bourbon—aged six years and 86 proof according to this billboard—was introduced to the market in 1939, joining a host of other brands produced at the distillery. Some of the brands produced were Cream of Kentucky, Echo Springs, Old Stagg, Carlisle, Three Feathers, and Buffalo Springs. That year was a high point for the distillery, with employment reaching 1,000. Unfortunately, World War II was just around the corner. (Authors' collection.)

HIS NOSE KNOWS. The "bouquet" of maturing bourbon is important to master distillers, and Buffalo Trace's Elmer T. Lee is one of the experts. Lee retired from active duty at the distillery in 1985 but in his role as "Master Distiller Emeritus" remains involved. He was credited with the idea when the distillery introduced the world's first single-barrel bourbon in 1984. It was named Blanton's in honor of Colonel Blanton. (Courtesy of Buffalo Trace Distillery.)

LOOKING FOR LEAKS. Former Buffalo Trace Distillery warehouse supervisor Jimmy Johnson checks the barrels in one of the warehouses for leaks. Now retired, Johnson returned to the distillery in 2008 to roll out Buffalo Trace's six-millionth barrel of bourbon. He has helped to roll out each millionth barrel since Prohibition. Each new milestone barrel replaces its predecessor in Warehouse V—the world's only one-barrel warehouse. (Courtesy of Buffalo Trace Distillery.)

HARD AT WORK. The Buffalo Trace Distillery site encompasses 118 acres and 114 buildings. The George T. Stagg Distillery was renamed Buffalo Trace in June 1999, and its flagship bourbon, Buffalo Trace Kentucky Straight Bourbon Whiskey, was introduced in August 1999. Tours are available six days a week as well as a gift shop and the George T. Stagg Gallery, which gives visitors a glimpse of the distillery's history. (Courtesy of Buffalo Trace Distillery.)

FOLLOW THE BUFFALO. Before the pioneers began to settle Kentucky, huge herds of buffalo carved out paths or "traces" through the virgin wilderness. The Great Buffalo Trace led some of the early settlers to a wide clearing created by the buffalo along the Kentucky River. It became the site of the Leestown settlement, and there has been a working distillery on the grounds since 1787. (Courtesy of Buffalo Trace Distillery.)

MASTER DISTILLER. Harlen Wheatley is one of the youngest of the current master distillers at the distilleries along Kentucky's Bourbon Trail but has extensive and wide-ranging experience in the distilling business. He took over from Gary Gayheart in 2005. All the master distillers at Buffalo Trace must be doing something right, since the distillery has won more international awards since 1990 than any other North American distillery. (Courtesy of Buffalo Trace Distillery.)

Five

FOUR ROSES

OLD PRENTICE DISTILLERY. The main building of today's Four Roses Distillery near Lawrenceburg was built in 1910 as Old Prentice Distillery. The mission-style architecture designed by Frankfort architect Leo Oberwarth is not often found in Kentucky. The property was listed on the National Register of Historic Places in 1987. The large bell seen in this early photograph was reportedly once a fire bell in Louisville. Its location is now unknown. (Courtesy of Four Roses Distillery.)

WHERE OLD JOE PEYTON PITCHED HIS TENT IN 1818.

WHERE "OLD JOE" MADE WHISKEY. It was in 1818 that pioneer "Old Joe" Peyton pitched his tent near the mouth of Gilbert's Creek on the Salt River and soon commenced to making whiskey at a site that would see many distilleries. Peyton's still grew and was acquired by Capt. Wiley Searcy in 1886. That distillery is pictured here around 1900 and produced Old Joe whiskey, considered bourbon's oldest brand, since 1818. (Courtesy of Kentucky Historical Society.)

EARLY OLD PRENTICE DISTILLERY. Around 1905, J. T. S. Brown and Sons, makers of Old Prentice and other brands, acquired this large facility on the banks of the Salt River. This photograph shows the "barrel track" that workmen used to roll barrels full of bourbon from the distillery to the seven-story rickhouse. The Old Prentice brand had been around since 1855. (Courtesy of Four Roses Distillery.)

HAULING COAL FOR DISTILLERY. Coal was the fuel that kept the steam boilers needed by bourbon distilleries going in the 1890s, when this image was made. Old Prentice would have used quite a bit to keep the mash tubs, stills, steam engines, and heaters going. The coal was probably transported from the nearby Kentucky River and up the hill daily by this team and driver. (Courtesy of Four Roses Distillery.)

MAIN BUILDING. J. T. S. Brown and Sons produced Old Prentice and Old Joe Whiskey in this facility (the warehouse seen in the previous picture at left) for many years. In 1910, they built the present-day mission-style distillery across the Bonds Mill Road. It's not clear when or why this older facility was destroyed. (Courtesy of Four Roses Distillery.)

FIRST LADY OF BOURBON. The new Old Prentice Distillery, eventually Four Roses, was built next to Montrose, the palatial home of Davis and Agnes Brown. After Davis Brown's death, Agnes Brown (seen here on the right with a friend) managed the Old Prentice organization and is believed to be the first woman in Kentucky to run a distillery. (Courtesy of Four Roses Distillery.)

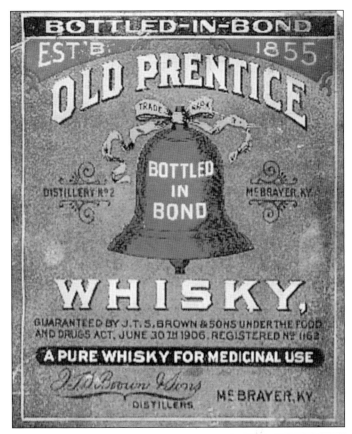

"**For Medicinal Use.**" During Prohibition, 1920–1933, J. T. S. Brown and Sons was allowed to sell some of its already warehoused Old Prentice through a special license held by Frankfort Distilleries for "Medicinal Use." This label gives the location of the distillery as "McBrayer, KY," the nearest post office to the facility. (Courtesy of Four Roses Distillery.)

300,000 Barrels. The Paul Jones Company's Frankfort Distillers continued to produce Old Joe and Old Prentice at the Bonds Mill Road location, as this photograph of the 300,000th barrel of Old Prentice in 1941 indicates. Frankfort Distillers and its many brands, including Four Roses, were sold to Joseph E. Seagram and Sons in 1943. (Courtesy of Four Roses Distilleries.)

DISTILLING ROOM. This image, taken after Prohibition, shows the distilling apparatus at the Bonds Mill Road site. The major sign reads "Old Joe Whiskies Since 1818" and shows, from left to right, the beer still (capacity 2,818 gallons), the "low wine" and "whisky" condensers, and the "doubler." (Courtesy of Four Roses Distillery.)

MASH VATS. This photograph was made in 1940 and is labeled as being at the "Old Joe Distillery at Bonds Mill." It shows workers preparing the yeast mixture to be added to the mash vats behind them. (Courtesy of Kentucky Historical Society.)

WHAT'S IN A NAME? How the Four Roses brand got its name and who owned it when are some of the many enigmas found in bourbon lore. The most romantic version regarding the name is the one presented in this 1935 magazine advertisement created when Frankfort Distilleries owned the brand. It relates the story of a beautiful Southern belle who signifies her acceptance of a marriage proposal by wearing a corsage of four roses. Regarding ownership, we know that the name and brand originated in Atlanta before the Civil War and were brought to Kentucky by Paul Jones Jr., who first trademarked them in August 1888. The name and brand were sold to Seagram by Frankfort Distilling in 1943. Many feel that Seagram almost destroyed the Four Roses name when they removed Four Roses Kentucky Straight Bourbon from the American market and replaced it with Four Roses American blended whiskey. The Japanese Kirin Brewery Company bought the brand in 2002 and has returned to making several excellent, premium Four Roses bourbons for the domestic and international markets. (Courtesy of Four Roses Distillery.)

MASTER DISTILLER. Jim Rutledge has more than 40 years' experience in the distilling industry and has been master distiller at Four Roses since 1995. He is a member of the inaugural class of the Bourbon Hall of Fame. His distillery is unique in that he uses two different mashbills (grain recipes) and five proprietary yeast cultures, hence 10 different recipes that are aged in separate barrels and used to create different renditions. (Courtesy of Four Roses Distillery.)

FOUR ROSES TODAY. The pale-yellow Four Roses' main building is one of the popular stops on the Kentucky Bourbon Trail. Tours include a Visitors Center with a video presentation, gift shop, and a taste of this historic bourbon for those old enough. (Courtesy of Four Roses Distillery.)

Six

HEAVEN HILL

BRAND NEW. Heaven Hill Distilleries, originally known as Old Heavenhill Springs Distillery, was established in 1934 near Bardstown by a group of investors, including the five Shapira brothers. Today it is an independent, family-owned business—the largest family-owned and -operated distillery in the country. Initially, the mashing capacity was 500 bushels of grain per day. Whiskey has been distilled in and around Bardstown since the town's founding in 1780. (Courtesy of Heaven Hill Distilleries, Inc.)

NAMED FOR WILLIAM HEAVENHILL. The name Heaven Hill comes from William Heavenhill, who once owned the land where the distillery was built. According to legend, William was born under a waterfall during an Indian raid in 1783. A clerical error turned Heavenhill into Heaven Hill when the distillery's name was changed from Old Heavenhill Springs Distillery in 1946. The name has remained Heaven Hill ever since. (Courtesy of Heaven Hill Distilleries, Inc.)

DEPRESSION-ERA START. The Old Heavenhill Springs Distillery started small with only 12 employees during the height of the Depression—the first barrel was filled on Friday, December 13, 1935. Twenty years later, the company produced its 500,000th barrel. All five Shapira brothers helped mark that September 30, 1955, milestone. From left to right are Ed Shapira, associate Charlie DeSpain, David Shapira, Mose Shapira, George Shapira, and Gary Shapira. (Courtesy of Heaven Hill Distilleries, Inc.)

EARLY DAYS. This painting shows several large warehouses (or rickhouses) and the distillery complex in Bardstown. Heaven Hill does not regulate the temperature in its warehouses; they rely on Mother Nature for warmth and cold that forces the bourbon to move in and out of the charred area inside the barrel, which helps produce the bourbon's taste and color. (Courtesy of Heaven Hill Distilleries, Inc.)

WATER SOURCE. Parker Beam checks out one of the sources for the water that is an important ingredient in bourbon-making, along with mashed grains and yeast. The water from the Heavenhill Spring has been impounded into a man-made lake. At one point, the lake was stocked with fish, and there was an official Heaven Hill Fishing Club with free lifetime memberships. (Courtesy of Heaven Hill Distilleries, Inc.)

CHECKING ALL THE DETAILS. Master distillers Parker Beam and his father, Earl Beam, check out the progress on the day's batch of bourbon. Earl Beam was the son of Park Beam—"Jim" Beam's brother. Earl was the first in the family to serve as master distiller at Heaven Hill, and he passed the job along to Parker in 1975. Parker's son Craig joined his father in 1983, and Parker and Craig Beam are now the distillery's master distillers. They are responsible not only for insuring that the bourbon produced at the distillery today is consistent with what has been made in the past, but also for the hundreds of thousands of barrels currently aging in more than 40 rickhouses throughout Nelson County. (Courtesy of Heaven Hill Distilleries, Inc.)

IMPORTANT STEP. The barrels that store the Heaven Hill bourbon are charred to a specified char level as part of the production process at the cooperages the company uses. The 53-gallon barrels are made of white oak staves, and the charring comes in several levels—another decision for the master distiller. The origin of the barrel charring that gives the bourbon its lovely color has been lost. (Courtesy of Heaven Hill Distilleries, Inc.)

ROLL OUT THE BARRELS. The finished barrels of bourbon are adjusted for alcohol content, weighed, tabulated, and moved to the rickhouses to begin the long, lazy wait until the master distillers decide they are ready to be emptied and their contents bottled. Distillers usually feel that the bourbon from the barrels aged in the upper stories is preferable to bourbon from barrels aged on the lower floors. (Courtesy of Heaven Hill Distilleries, Inc.)

ANOTHER BARREL IN THE RICKHOUSE. The taste of the finished product depends on several factors, including the placement of the barrel in the rickhouse, the seasonal variations in temperature during the barrel's stay in the rickhouse, and the number of years that the barrel stays there. The Heaven Hill Distilleries' rickhouses currently contain more than 800,000 barrels of gently aging bourbon—the second largest holding in the world. (Courtesy of Heaven Hill Distilleries, Inc.)

AGING IS GOOD. Thousands of barrels of bourbon are maturing in the rickhouses at Heaven Hill Distilleries. The bourbon moves in and out of the charred inside of the barrels, picking up various flavors for several years as it matures. The portion of the bourbon that evaporates during aging is called the "angel's share." (Courtesy of Heaven Hill Distilleries, Inc.)

A 1999 PURCHASE. After the 1996 fire that destroyed the distillery and seven rickhouses, Heaven Hill temporarily made bourbon at several other distilleries using the Heaven Hill yeast, proprietary mashbill, and process. In 1999, the company purchased the Bernheim Distillery in Louisville but kept its corporate headquarters, storage, bottling, and distribution facilities in Bardstown. As part of that sale, Heaven Hill also acquired the Old Fitzgerald bourbon brand. (Courtesy of Heaven Hill Distilleries, Inc.)

BOURBON HERITAGE CENTER. Heaven Hill's Bourbon Heritage Center, 2009 winner of the "Visitor Attraction of the Year" award from *Whisky Magazine*, can be seen here between bonded rickhouses. It opened in 2004 and welcomes nearly 50,000 people a year to the Bardstown area. The black mold that can be seen near the bottom of the rickhouses is a natural by-product of the bourbon aging process. (Courtesy of Heaven Hill Distilleries, Inc.)

BOURBON TASTING BARREL. One of the features of the Bourbon Heritage Center is a large circular tasting room built to resemble the inside of a wooden bourbon barrel. Here visitors can taste different brands of bourbon produced by Heaven Hill under the tutelage of bourbon tasting experts. Heaven Hill's brands include Elijah Craig, Evan Williams, Henry McKenna, Fighting Cock, and Old Fitzgerald. (Courtesy of Heaven Hill Distilleries, Inc.)

BORN TO BE MASTER DISTILLERS. Craig Beam (left) joined his father, Parker, at Heaven Hill Distilleries in 1983 as the seventh generation of his family to enter the distilling business. Both master distillers, they keep busy with the expanded Bernheim distillery and the 35 million gallons of bourbon maturing in the rickhouses. The 2008 edition of Parker's Heritage Collection was named "American Whiskey of the Year" by *Malt Advocate Magazine*. (Courtesy of Heaven Hill Distilleries, Inc.)

Seven

JIM BEAM

JUST A TASTE. James "Jim" B. Beam was given the reins to the family distillery in 1894. He was the great-grandson of Jacob Beam, who sold his first barrel of Kentucky whiskey in 1795 and began a distilling dynasty. Here Jim is pictured getting a drink from his assistant distiller, Bill Douglas. The Beam family has provided distillery owners and employees, including master distillers, for more than two centuries. (Courtesy of Jim Beam Brands Company.)

OLD TUB
⊹ SALOON ⊹

I have for sale BOONE & BRO.'s Three-year-old. Strictly Pure, 40c. per quart.

Also F. G. Walker's "QUEEN OF NELSON" Four-year-old, 50c per quart.

OLD · TUB · WHISKY

Three years and up, 60 to 75c per quart, guaranteed Strictly Pure, just as it is when taken from bonded warehouse.

Keeps the best brand of Brandies, Wines, Cigars, Tobacco; also ice cold Beer and Ale.

T. D. BEAM, Prop.

POPULAR DURING CIVIL WAR. Jacob Beam's original Old Jake Beam's Sour Mash gave way to Old Tub Whisky in the 1850s. In 1859, David M. Beam, Jacob Beam's grandson, moved the Beam brand from its original home in Washington County to nearby Bardstown to take advantage of the Louisville and Nashville rail extension that was being built there. Old Tub was reportedly the most popular bourbon in Kentucky during the Civil War. (Courtesy of Dixie Hibbs.)

LOTS OF BEAMS. Jacob Beam, the founder of the Kentucky distilling dynasty, and his wife, Mary, began the tradition of having large families with a brood of 12 children. The family has grown exponentially for eight generations. Pictured here is a load of Beams on a trip to Mammoth Cave more than a century ago. (Courtesy of Jim Beam Brands Company.)

THE BEAMS AT HOME. This photograph, taken about 1912, shows Jim Beam; his son T. Jeremiah; his wife, Mary; daughters Mildred and Margaret (Noe); Jim Beam's father, David M. Beam; and his brother William Park Beam. Their home, on Bardstown's "Distillers Row" on North Third Street, had once been a part of the Bardstown Female Academy, or Roseland Academy. Jim Beam died here, peacefully, on Christmas morning of 1947 of a heart ailment. Jim and Mary Mae Beam were married for more than 50 years. Members of the Beam family still live in the home. (Courtesy of Jim Beam Brands Company.)

BEAM'S CLERMONT HOUSE. When the Beams reentered the bourbon business immediately after Prohibition, they built their new distillery on property in Clermont in nearby Bullitt County. The site had been the home of the Old Murphy Barber Distillery from 1891 to 1913. This house was built in 1911, and T. Jeremiah Beam, Jim Beam's son, moved in during 1933. The house is on the National Register of Historic Places. (Courtesy of Jim Beam Brands Company.)

BEAM GENERATIONS. This photograph from the 1960s shows, from left to right, T. Jeremiah Beam, Booker Noe, Baker Beam, and David Beam, all direct descendants of the Kentucky pioneer distiller Jacob Beam. (Courtesy of Jim Beam Brands Company.)

JIM BEAM. Born in 1864, the last full year of the Civil War, James "Jim" Beauregard Beam worked in the family's business all of his adult life. His great distilling knowledge and business acumen guided the family into the 20th century, rebuilt the business after Prohibition, and made the Jim Beam brand the most successful bourbon in the world. His distilling peers elected him as president of the Kentucky Distillers' Association in 1916. He is pictured here in his Clermont office in 1945, two years before his death. He was often described as "quiet," "a gentleman," and "a genius." (Courtesy of Oscar Getz Museum of Whiskey History.)

MASTER DISTILLER AND SMOKED HAM MASTER. Frederick Booker Noe II was born in 1929, the son of Jim Beam's daughter Margaret Noe and therefore grandson of the famous Jim Beam himself. Besides becoming one of bourbon's finest distillers and possibly the industry's premier ambassador, he loved to cure hams, another traditional Kentucky product, in a backyard smokehouse. (Courtesy of Jim Beam Brands Company.)

SIXTH-GENERATION DISTILLER. Frederick Booker Noe II served as a master distiller for Jim Beam Brands for more than 40 years. He developed several "small batch" brands for the company. Upon his death in 2004, the *New York Times* wrote, "In 1988, with the creation of Booker's Bourbon, premium bourbon, he helped revitalize the bourbon business." This sculpture of Booker is at the Jim Beam distillery in Clermont. (Courtesy of Jim Beam Brands Company.)

"IN THE BLOOD." Frederick Booker Noe III, or "Fred," is the seventh-generation Beam to oversee the creation of Kentucky bourbons labeled "Beam." He personally selects the barrels for Booker's Bourbon and has served as a Bourbon Ambassador for Jim Beam and the Small Batch Bourbon Collection since 1999. As his father put it, "Tasting a Small Batch Bourbon is like tasting the past"—something the Beams know well. (Courtesy of Jim Beam Brands Company.)

AN ANCIENT ART. Kentucky bourbon, and other distilled spirits, are the product of fermentation followed by distillation in stills that boil the mixture. Alcohol boils at a lower temperature than water; the resulting vapors are collected and become "high wine." Pictured are the glass "tail boxes" at the Jim Beam Distillery where the crystal-clear "new bourbon whiskey" or "white dog" flows to be viewed by distillers before being barreled. (Courtesy of Jim Beam Brands Company.)

BARRELS OF BEAM. In 1965, the one-millionth barrel of Jim Beam since Prohibition was filled. In 2005, Fred Noe, Jim Beam's great-grandson, filled the 10-millionth barrel of Jim Beam at the Clermont distillery. Jim Beam Kentucky Straight Bourbon Whiskey is aged for four years in barrels like those seen in this photograph; Beam's Small Batch Collection of bourbons is aged between six and nine years. (Courtesy of Jim Beam Brands Company.)

AMERICAN OUTPOST. Nestled next to the less attractive industrial sprawl of Jim Beam's Clermont distillery is American Outpost. The visitor center is housed in a replica of an old tobacco barn and contains a museum, gift shop, and a theater where visitors watch a film about bourbon and Jim Beam. Next door is the 1911 Beam family home where visitors may enjoy the taste of the Small Batch Bourbon Collection. (Courtesy of Jim Beam Brands Company.)

Eight

MAKER'S MARK

NATIONALLY RECOGNIZED SITE.
The National Park Service
granted the Maker's Mark
Distillery site National Historic
Landmark status in 1980,
recognizing it as the "oldest
Kentucky distillery site still
in use." Charles Burks built
a distillery here along with
a gristmill around 1805 and
operated it until 1831. Some of
the present buildings were built
by his grandson in 1889 when he
restarted the distillery. (Courtesy
of Maker's Mark Distillery.)

LOTS OF WORK. In 1953, Bill Samuels Sr. bought and restored a small distillery in Loretto, founding Maker's Mark Distillery. Today, carefully keeping with its Victorian style, the Samuels family has built a visitor's tasting room; rebuilt the tollhouse, which serves bourbon-inspired dishes for lunch; refurbished the master distiller's home; and is restoring the centuries-old, hand-laid rock fences that add character to the site. (Courtesy of Maker's Mark Distillery.)

BURKS' HOUSE. This beautiful Victorian house sits on a hill overlooking the distillery and was home to the original family who developed the site that has produced milled grains, spring water, wine, and distilled whiskey over two centuries. Located in an area known as Happy Hollow, the property also boasts a 10-acre lake of limestone spring water. Every drop of Maker's Mark is made with the pure iron-free water. (Courtesy of Maker's Mark Distillery.)

ONE WHISKEY
ONE QUALITY

T. W. SAMUELS

KENTUCKY
STRAIGHT
BOURBON
WHISKEY

T.W.SAMUELS

STRAIGHT
BOURBON
WHISKEY

ONE whiskey, one quality, tells the story, Leslie B. Samuels and T. W. Samuels devoting their entire time to the production of T. W. SAMUELS —made the same as their forefathers made it 90 years ago, and as they have made it ever since.

T. W. SAMUELS Straight Kentucky Bourbon, made in Nelson Co., as it was in pre-prohibition days, no artificial, or quick aging. We are particularly proud of our new plant. Modern warehouses are constructed mostly of glass, insuring a quality whiskey of unusual maturity.

"There's a barrel of satisfaction in every bottle"

T. W. SAMUELS
STRAIGHT BOURBON WHISKEY

Distilled and Bottled by T. W. SAMUELS DISTILLERY, Inc.
DISTILLERY — DEATSVILLE (NELSON CO.) KY.
Executive Offices: 404-406 KEITH BUILDING, CINCINNATI

T. W. SAMUELS BRAND. At the end of Prohibition in 1933, Leslie Samuels, the grandson of T. W. Samuels, re-launched the family's bourbon whiskey. The drink's slogan was, "There's a barrel of satisfaction in every bottle." Taylor Williams Samuels was the first in the family to incorporate the family distillery into a "real business" about 1840 and was also among the first to brand his whiskey, calling it T. W. Samuels. As Nelson County's high sheriff, he presided over possibly the final surrender of the Civil War at the family distillery in Samuels, Kentucky. (Courtesy of Maker's Mark Distillery.)

IN SEARCH OF SOMETHING NEW. In 1952, after six generations and nearly 170 years, Bill Samuels Sr. wanted a new taste for his family's bourbon whiskey, one that wasn't "harsh and bitter." By using various combinations of grains in baking breads, Samuels discovered that the sweet winter red wheat produced the smoothest taste. As his son, Bill Jr., remembers, "We ate a lot of bread during that time." (Courtesy of Maker's Mark Distillery.)

REALLY A FAMILY BUSINESS. While Bill Samuels Sr. founded Maker's Mark in 1953 and developed the bourbon's unique taste, it was his wife, Margie, who created the design for the bottle and came up with the name. Their son, Bill Jr., took over as president of the company in 1975. This family portrait shows Bill Sr., Bill Jr., and Margie holding Leslie and Nancy (right). (Courtesy of Maker's Mark Distillery.)

THE FIRST BOTTLE OF MAKER'S. Bill Samuels Sr.'s biggest change in the family's distilling recipe was replacing rye as the "flavor grain" with red winter wheat for a gentler, smoother taste. He made the first batch in 1953, and it was ready to bottle in 1958. His wife, Margie, who was an amateur calligrapher, designed the unique squared bottle and created the typeface for the label. As a collector of cognac bottles, she also came up with the idea of dipping the bottles in the now iconic red wax and allowing the tendrils to drip down the sides. Margie was a serious collector of old pewter, where the "maker's mark" was an important element, and therefore suggested the new bourbon's name. Thus, she is one of the few women to make a major contribution to the industry. The Samuelses also decided to break away from the American spelling and return to the Scotch-Irish spelling of "whisky," which denoted that this bourbon was made in small manageable batches of no more that 1,000 gallons each, about 19 barrels. (Courtesy of Maker's Mark Distillery.)

BOURBON DYNASTIES UNDER SAME TENT. The intertwined family roots of many Kentucky distilling dynasties are illustrated in this charming early photograph of the Samuels children playing with some of the Beam children growing up near Bardstown. In the small world of Kentucky bourbon-making, some connections come from marriage, some from lifelong friendships. Bourbon distillers may be competitors but are foremost friends who will drop everything to help another distiller. (Courtesy of Maker's Mark Distillery.)

FROM FATHER TO SON. Bill Samuels Jr. (left) became president and chief executive officer of Maker's Mark in 1975. After he studied engineering (and helped design the first non-graphite rocket nozzle for the Polaris missile), then graduated from Vanderbilt Law School, Bill Jr.'s natural ability for marketing and promotion is generally credited with Maker's commercial success. He is pictured here with his son Rob, the eighth generation of this distilling family. (Courtesy of Maker's Mark Distillery.)

Every Bottle is Hand-Dipped. All bottles of Maker's Mark are hand-dipped at the Loretto distillery. Visitors of legal drinking age can even hand dip their own bottle of Maker's Mark in the distillery's gift gallery. While most bottles are dipped in the famous red wax, there are some exceptions, including two charity series, Keeneland and Turfway. These unique partnerships between racetracks and a distillery have raised millions for Kentucky-area charities. (Courtesy of Maker's Mark Distillery.)

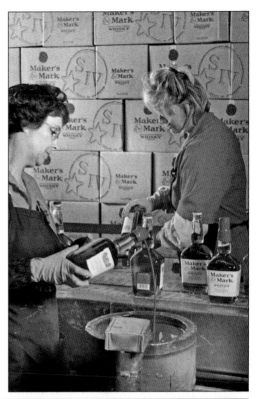

On *CBS Sunday Morning Show*. Master distiller Kevin Smith shows CBS senior correspondent Martha Teichner some of the finer points of bourbon-making at Maker's Mark for a 2008 segment of the *CBS Sunday Morning Show*. Smith has over 20 years of bourbon industry experience and oversees the handmade production of Maker's Mark from the selection of grains to choosing the white oak barrels and the final bourbon tasting. (Courtesy of Maker's Mark Distillery.)

LANDMARK AND TOURIST ATTRACTION. The "little country distillery" that became the home of Maker's Mark in 1953 has become one of Kentucky's major tourist attractions. It is the only distillery that has the entire process on site, from grain to bottle, and a free informative tour is given every day except on major holidays. The site also features a gift shop, a tasting room, and a restaurant. (Courtesy of Maker's Mark Distillery.)

OLDEST LIQUOR STORE. The old "quart house" at the Maker's Mark facility was built around 1889 and is believed to be America's oldest remaining "retail package store." It is authentically restored to reflect the era well before Prohibition, when neighbors came with their quart jars and jugs to have them filled from whiskey casks there. (Courtesy of Maker's Mark Distillery.)

Nine

WILD TURKEY

HOME OF WILD TURKEY. For years, motorists crossing the Kentucky River on the Tyrone Bridge from Woodford County into Anderson County have stared up the hill into the home of Kentucky bourbon's "Kickin' Chicken," Wild Turkey Distillery. The hill has been the home of award-winning bourbon distilleries since the Ripy brothers built here in 1905. Austin Nichols and Company brought the Wild Turkey brand here in 1970. (Courtesy of Wild Turkey Distillery.)

A DISTILLING DYNASTY. In 1869, Thomas B. Ripy and his partner, W. H. McBrayer, bought a small Anderson County distillery on the banks of the Kentucky River in a town named Tyrone. They made T. B. Ripy Sour Mash there and along with other distilleries made Tyrone one of the state's busy and prosperous river towns. In 1905, Ripy's four sons established Ripy Brothers Distillers on the hill where Wild Turkey now stands. (Courtesy of Ripy Family Collection.)

RIPY FAMILY ON VACATION. Like many Kentucky families of their time, especially distilling ones, the Ripys enjoyed large, close families. T. B. Ripy is seen here in 1890 with his family enjoying French Lick Springs, a popular Indiana resort. Ripys continue to work in the bourbon business today. (Courtesy of Ripy Family Collection.)

PROHIBITION'S "NOBLE EXPERIMENT." America's great social and legal blunder began on January 17, 1920. Although much of Kentucky's warehoused bourbon would be sold for "medicinal use," only a small amount of legal bourbon distilling was allowed in the state. Hundreds of distilleries in many counties were closed forever, and thousands of workers were out of work just as the world's Great Depression was beginning. The early days of Prohibition created a few enthusiastic photo opportunities like this one, showing cases of Old Ripy and Old Taylor being put to the axe. Prohibition ended on December 5, 1933, and the Ripys and other distilling families returned to the business. However, many small distilleries couldn't succeed during the coming age of "big business." (Courtesy of Ripy Family Collection.)

OLD BRAND IN NEW LOCATION. The J. T. S. Brown label had been around 100 years when the owners moved it to the old Ripy plant in 1955. In this 1960s photograph, J. T. S. Brown employees Billy Noel, Orville Robinson, Charles Buntain, Chink Moore, Ike Case, Mike Adams, and Jim McGinnis are seen in the filling and weighing room. (Courtesy of Ripy Family Collection.)

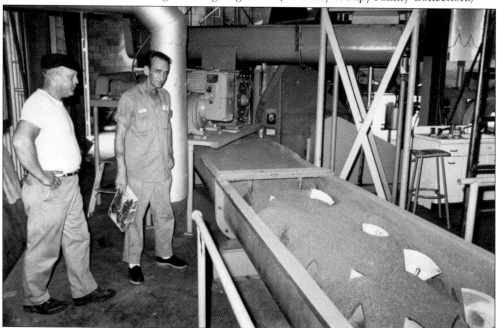

GRAIN ROOM. In this photograph, Willie Bryant (left) and Joe Noel are keeping an eye on the grain drying and blending process for the "mash bill." Wild Turkey has a lower percentage of corn in its recipe than any other brand in the bourbon industry, using more premium rye and malted barley for its robust taste. (Courtesy of Wild Turkey Distillers.)

STACKING BARRELS. Since law requires that bourbon can only be aged in new oak barrels, old barrels must find another home. In this 1950s photograph, J. T. S. Brown workers can be seen stacking the used barrels an ominous 13 levels high before they were shipped out for other uses. Some went to producers of other distilled spirits, including whisky distillers in the British Isles. (Courtesy of Wild Turkey Distillers.)

MEMORABLE BARREL.
E. W. Ripy Jr. (left) and Orville Robinson are seen here in 1961 with the 400,000th barrel of J. T. S. Brown made in Anderson County. The J. T. S. Brown label has been around since 1870, when John Thompson Street Brown introduced it in Louisville. It was made by the Ripys from 1950 until the late 1970s. It is now made by Heaven Hill in Bardstown. (Courtesy of Ripy Family Collection.)

BOURBON-MASH FED. Thomas Beebe Ripy is seen here with a large buffalo fish, *Ictiobus cyprinellus*, which he caught in the Kentucky River near an outlet that discharged some of the Tyrone distilleries' used mash in the 1950s. Environmental concerns no longer allow the dumping of what must be a delightful treat for the river's fish. (Courtesy of Ripy Family Collection.)

HUGE MASH TUBS. Giant cypress mash tubs with capacities of over 155,000 gallons are where the fermentation process takes place. Before the Civil War, distilleries used hundreds, even thousands of small tubs that were hand stirred to mix the mashbill, water, and yeast that creates the "distillers beer," which is distilled. This 1960s photograph shows Mark Adams watching the bubbling brew. (Courtesy of Wild Turkey Distillery.)

WAREHOUSING, BOTTLING, AND SHIPPING. Today's Wild Turkey Distillery is a sprawling facility dominated by giant wood-frame and metal-clad warehouses. The barrels of newly distilled spirits are placed in the unheated warehouses for their four- to 12-year stay there. (Courtesy of Wild Turkey Distillery.)

CONSISTENT QUALITY. Master Distiller James "Jimmy" Russell has been working at the Wild Turkey Distillery for more than 50 years, since the age of 19. He is responsible for keeping the "Kickin' Chicken" made in "the old-fashion way." Russell favors his bourbon "heavy with taste" and prefers Wild Turkey barrels to be charred to the darkest degree. He is shown here when he created Wild Turkey Rare Breed brand. (Courtesy of Wild Turkey Distillery.)

FATHER TO SON. For nearly 30 years, Eddie Russell has followed his father around Wild Turkey's distillery and many warehouses, learning the complex distiller's trade. Under his father's tutelage, he has learned how to carry the traditions and knowledge of his skilled father into the 21st century. (Courtesy of Wild Turkey Distillery.)

Ten

WOODFORD RESERVE

EVERYONE TURNED OUT. Photography was still in its infancy in 1883, and everyone wanted to get in the picture. This photograph of the Labrot and Graham distillery crew (many holding their tools of the trade) includes everyone from the co-owners to the little boys who were probably always underfoot. In the first row, Leopold Labrot is the third from the left and James Graham is fourth from left. (Courtesy of Kentucky Historical Society.)

"OLD OSCAR PEPPER" DISTILLERY,

WOODFORD COUNTY, KENTUCKY.

LABROT & GRAHAM, PROPRIETORS.

LOTS OF BOURBON MADE HERE. By the time this photograph was taken in 1883, whiskey had already been made on the site for more than 70 years. The distillery was founded in 1812 in Woodford County on the banks of the Grassy Spring branch of Glenn's Creek by Elijah Pepper. Elijah's son Oscar hired Dr. James Crow as master distiller in 1833. Dr. Crow was a chemist, and for the next 19 years, he worked to develop scientific methods to ensure that the taste of the bourbon was uniform from batch to batch. He accomplished this by inventing the "sour mash" process, in which some of the previous batch is set back for use in the next batch. In a *Louisville Times* interview in 1909, Col. E. H. Taylor Jr. said, "I remember when James Crow, whom I knew, gave us the first practical use of the hydrometer, saccharometer, thermometer, etc. which inaugurated a new basis toward systematic procedure in the distillation of Kentucky whiskey." The distillery underwent several ownership changes and is now the Woodford Reserve Distillery, owned by Brown-Forman Corporation. (Courtesy of Kentucky Historical Society.)

VINTNER TURNED DISTILLER.
Leopold Labrot was a French wine
producer who came to America in
1870. His background as a vintner
probably helped him learn the
whiskey distilling business quickly
at Frankfort's Hermitage Distillery.
He and James Graham bought the
Oscar Pepper distillery in 1878,
and a partnership by the name of
Labrot and Graham continued
to operate it until 1941, except
during Prohibition years. In an
1888 trade publication, his surname
was spelled La Brot. (Courtesy of
Brown-Forman Corporation.)

FRANKFORT MERCHANT. James
Graham was of Irish descent.
The partnership he formed with
Labrot controlled the distillery
for more than 50 years but
was finally forced to sell out in
1941 after the U.S. government
banned all whiskey-making for
the duration of World War II.
The distillery was sold to Brown-
Forman, which eventually sold it
and later repurchased it in 1994 to
produce the premium Woodford
Reserve bourbon. (Courtesy of
Brown-Forman Corporation.)

WHERE IT ALL HAPPENED. This distillery building with the "L&G" on the smokestacks contained the complete distilling process from the arrival of the grain to the departure of the filled barrels of bourbon on their way to a warehouse via the longest barrel run ever used in a distillery. It allowed a man to easily roll a 500-pound barrel from the distillery to any of the warehouses. (Courtesy of Brown-Forman Corporation.)

NEAT AS A PIN. These women on the bottling line in the stone bottling house at Labrot and Graham's Old Oscar Pepper Distillery in their clean white shirtwaists and matching bows illustrate the cleanliness of the bottling process. Bottling became popular after the Bottled-in-Bond Act of 1897 was passed. The man in the hat is probably a government official, as all steps of the bourbon-making process were monitored by the government. (Courtesy of Brown-Forman Corporation.)

DON'T LOSE THE RECEIPT. Individuals and businesses could "invest" in barrels of bourbon stored in bonded warehouses at distilleries. They could make a profit when the bourbon was bottled and sold after all taxes and storage costs were paid, and the money the distillery owners received helped pay the burdensome taxes. This 1917 receipt is for five barrels of Old Oscar Pepper Sour Mash. (Courtesy of Brown-Forman Corporation.)

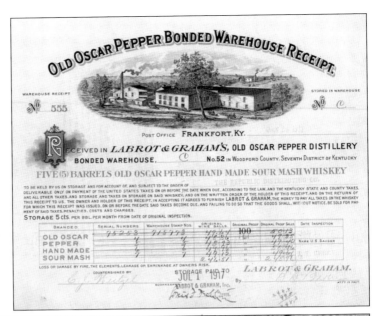

DISTILLERY WORKERS, 1935. After the repeal of Prohibition, which lasted from 1920 until 1933, it wasn't long before the Labrot and Graham Distillery was back up and running again. The distillery underwent extensive renovations and was running at full capacity by 1935. By 1938, there were 57 operating distilleries in Kentucky employing more than 7,500 people. Unfortunately, no one knew that further restrictions were just around the corner. (Courtesy of Brown-Forman Corporation.)

INNOVATOR IN THE 1860s. George Garvin Brown was a pharmaceuticals salesman in Louisville. One of the most popular "medicines" he sold was whiskey, which was prescribed for a variety of maladies. He decided to offer a solution to complaints from doctors that the product that reached their patients had often been adulterated. In 1870, he and his brother J. T. S. Brown started a company to sell bourbon in sealed glass bottles. Brown-Forman is the only Kentucky distilling company predating Prohibition that is still controlled by its founding family. (Courtesy of Brown-Forman Corporation.)

MEDICINAL WHISKEY. This wagon delivered Old Forester Whiskey, the flagship brand of the partnership formed by George Garvin Brown and his brother. The company went through several name changes and eventually became Brown-Forman. Old Forester was originally spelled "Forrester" because of the fact that it was endorsed by Dr. William Forrester, a Civil War hero and a leading physician in Louisville. Old Forrester Straight Bourbon Whiskey was the first product sold in sealed bottles. (Courtesy of Brown-Forman Corporation.)

A 1904 OFFICE. While photographs of distillery crews are more common, much of the work done at early distilleries involved paperwork—keeping track of the thousands of gallons of bourbon maturing in warehouses and paying all the taxes took lots of manpower (and womanpower). Things are different today, with computers taking on much of what used to be done by hand. George Garvin Brown is seated at far right. (Courtesy of Brown-Forman Corporation.)

LOTS OF DIFFICULT DECISIONS. When George Garvin Brown's oldest son, Owsley (seated), took over the company in 1917, he couldn't have foreseen the difficult times ahead for the family business. He guided Brown-Forman through two World Wars, Prohibition, and the Great Depression. During Prohibition, Brown received one of only 10 licenses granted by the federal government to bottle whiskey for medicinal purposes in order to utilize their stocks of Old Forester. (Courtesy of Brown-Forman Corporation.)

EARLY TIMES PURCHASED. Brown-Forman purchased the Early Times Distillery and its entire barreled stock in 1923 during Prohibition and moved it to their warehouses in Louisville in order to have enough bourbon on hand to continue bottling "medicinal whiskey." Early Times was founded in 1860 at Early Times Station, and this boxcar of their product was shipped to Utah in 1896. Early Times became the country's best-selling bourbon in 1953. (Courtesy of Brown-Forman Corporation.)

A LOUISVILLE LANDMARK. The company, under the guidance of the fifth generation of the Brown family, continues to make Old Forester, which is the only bourbon in existence today that was sold before, during, and after Prohibition. The 68-foot-high bottle of Old Forester on top of the building can be seen from almost anywhere in downtown Louisville and has a 100,000 gallon capacity—enough for 8.5 million generous portions of Old Forester. (Courtesy of Brown-Forman Corporation.)

A NEW DIRECTION. In the 1990s, the leadership at Brown-Forman became interested in producing a premium bourbon, and in 1994, they decided to repurchase the Labrot and Graham Distillery that they had sold in 1973. This photograph shows Brown-Forman engineer Forrest Tanner supervising the installation of a barrel batching tank in the bottling hall at Woodford Reserve. (Courtesy of Brown-Forman Corporation.)

COPPER POT STILLS. At the heart of the new, but traditional, distilling equipment installed at Woodford Reserve are the three copper pot stills made in Rothes, Scotland. The stills triple distill the mash in batches and not continuously like the newer column stills. The painstaking renovations to the historical distillery complex led to the Labrot and Graham Oscar Pepper Distillery site being named as a National Historic Landmark in 2000. (Courtesy of Brown-Forman Corporation.)

BARREL NUMBER ONE. Woodford Reserve bourbon was introduced in 1996 and has since won top honors at three of the industry's most important tasting competitions. In 2003, the distillery was officially renamed as the Woodford Reserve Distillery in honor of its bourbon label. Each step in Woodford Reserve's traditional distilling process is on display to the thousands of visitors who tour the facility. (Courtesy of Brown-Forman Corporation.)

EVERY BARREL TASTED. Every barrel of Woodford Reserve is tasted several times as it matures in the heated and cooled warehouses at the distillery. Brown-Forman's master distiller Chris Morris checks the bourbon's taste, aroma, and color, and only when he is completely satisfied is the bourbon in that barrel headed to the bottling room. Morris is only the seventh master distiller at Brown-Forman since the company started in 1870. (Courtesy of Brown-Forman Corporation.)

Eleven

TOM MOORE

AFTER PROHIBITION. This view of the Tom Moore Distillery near Bardstown was taken in the late 1930s, after Prohibition ended. By 1938, when the first bourbon made after Prohibition had matured for four years and was eligible to be bottled-in-bond, the Tom Moore Distillery was one of 58 distilleries operating in Kentucky. Those 58 plants represented a capital investment of $100 million and provided employment for 7,500 people. (Courtesy of Dixie Hibbs.)

First Distillery. In 1876, when Tom Moore was 23 years old, he and coworker Ben Mattingly bought the Nelson County plant known as the Willet, Frank, and Company Distillery and renamed it the Mattingly and Moore Distillery. The distillery's best-known brand at that time was Belle of Nelson, but in 1879, Tom Moore Bourbon was launched. It is still made today at the Tom Moore Distillery near Bardstown. (Courtesy of Dixie Hibbs.)

On His Own. Eventually, Moore moved a short distance south of the Mattingly and Moore Distillery to build the Tom Moore Distillery. According to an item in the 1889 *Wine and Spirits Bulletin*, "Tom Moore is one of the cleverest distillers in Kentucky, and makes a whiskey fine enough to set before a King." (Courtesy of Dixie Hibbs.)

LATER IN LIFE. Tom Moore is seen here (second from left) with his second wife, Nillie Simon Moore, and her brothers. Moore reopened his distillery at the end of Prohibition but only ran it for a few years before his death in 1937. The distillery went through several ownership changes before being purchased in 1943 by Oscar Getz, who changed the name to the Barton Distilling Company. (Courtesy of Oscar Getz Museum of Whiskey History.)

ATTRACTIVE LABEL. This attractive label for Tom Moore Kentucky Straight Bourbon Whiskey featuring a pair of horses is still in use today. The 1896 "Historical and Industrial Supplement" to the *Nelson County Record* described Tom Moore: "Chuck full of energy, prompt in everything, he is one of the best examples of a successful businessman in the county." (Courtesy of Oscar Getz Museum of Whiskey History.)

PROMOTIONAL PHOTOGRAPH. It looks like this young lady posing for a photograph, probably in the late 1940s or 1950s, likes what she sees. Tom Moore found a different way to market his product in 1896, according to a newspaper account: "Mr. Moore readily disposes of his product by sending samples to the trade, believing this to be the best way of showing the kind of goods he manufactures." (Courtesy of Oscar Getz Museum of Whiskey History.)

POSTCARD PERFECT. This postcard view of the Barton Distilling Company was probably taken in the 1960s. It shows the 180-acre property, including the largest distillery under one roof in Kentucky. According to the text on the back of the postcard, "Kentucky bourbon of the highest quality has been distilled, aged and bottled on these same premises since 1879." (Courtesy of Oscar Getz Museum of Whiskey History.)

MILESTONE BARREL. This photograph shows the management of the Barton Distilling Company with the distillery's two-millionth barrel. From left to right are Paul Kraus, Frank Kraus, and Oscar Getz. Getz collected historical whiskey-industry items and eventually displayed them in a museum at Barton Distilling Company. Located at first in a large trailer, the Barton Museum of Whiskey History was opened to the public in 1957. (Courtesy of Oscar Getz Museum of Whiskey History.)

MUSEUM AT EDGEWOOD. The Barton Museum of Whiskey History was later moved to Edgewood, a large Federal-style home in Bardstown. This photograph shows Mr. and Mrs. Oscar Getz welcoming a guest to Edgewood. After Getz's death, his widow, Emma Abelson Getz, donated the collection to the city of Bardstown, and it was moved to Spalding Hall. It was dedicated in 1984 as the Oscar Getz Museum of Whiskey History. (Courtesy of Oscar Getz Museum of Whiskey History.)

FAMOUS SPRING. One of the sites on the walking tour of the Tom Moore Distillery is the spring shown here. The sign celebrates the "never fail" spring and its importance to the success of the bourbon brands made at the distillery, especially Tom Moore Bourbon, which has been made since 1879 using the spring's water. The distillery was added to the Kentucky Bourbon Trail in 2008. (Courtesy of Tom Moore Distillery.)

GIANT BARREL. This 15-foot-high barrel on display at the Tom Moore Distillery was the brainchild of Steve Hayden, who wanted to honor the bourbon industry in Bardstown, which has the title of "Bourbon Capital of the World." Bardstown is the site of the Kentucky Bourbon Festival each September. The Tom Moore Distillery's walking tour showcases the distillery's bourbon-making process, from distilling to aging and bottling. (Courtesy of Tom Moore Distillery.)

SUPER PREMIUM BOURBON. The Tom Moore Distillery's small-batch premium 1792 Ridgemont Reserve Bourbon is aged for eight years. The bourbon's 1792 name refers to the year Kentucky became a state. It is the official toasting bourbon of the annual Kentucky Bourbon Festival. The distillery also produces several large-batch bourbons, including Very Old Barton, Kentucky Tavern, Kentucky Gentleman, and Ten High. (Courtesy of Tom Moore Distillery.)

YOUNGEST MASTER DISTILLER. Tom Moore's Greg Davis is currently the youngest master distiller in the bourbon industry. His take on the job of master distiller merges traditional distilling practices and a modern-day spirit. At the Bardstown distillery, Davis is responsible for the bourbon maturing in the warehouses and the nearly 600 barrels produced each day. (Courtesy of Tom Moore Distillery.)

www.arcadiapublishing.com

MAP SEARCH

Find Your Place in History.